AGING:
PROSPECTS AND ISSUES

A MONOGRAPH FROM THE
ETHEL PERCY ANDRUS GERONTOLOGY CENTER

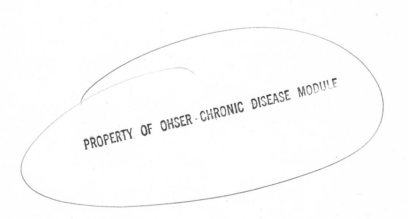

edited by

Richard H. Davis, Ph.D.
Director, Publications Office
and
Margaret Neiswender, Project Editor

Cover design by Victor Regnier

i

This monograph is composed of papers presented by outstanding authorities in the field of aging at a series of institutes sponsored by the Ethel Percy Andrus Gerontology Center of the University of Southern California. These institutes are part of the Continuing Professional Education in Aging Project supported by the National Institute of Mental Health (Grant No. MH 11440).

I   THE EXPERIENCE OF AGING

*James E. Birren, Ph.D.**

I have recently been given a grant from the Administration on Aging to revise the *Handbook on Aging* which I first published in 1959. We are now going to expand this project to include separate handbooks on the biology of aging, the psychology of aging and a handbook on social gerontology. It will require these three handbooks to summarize what we have learned in the last ten years. It will take us about three years to write these books. A man I respect very much once told me that there is a lag of 15 years from the time something is learned in the laboratory until it becomes standard in the textbooks. I think the lag is shorter than that today. We no longer have to wait for the textbook. Some of what the contributors to this monograph are saying comes straight from the laboratory and hasn't been published yet.

It has been observed that about eighty percent of the elderly are women. Is this an illustration of social regression where aging is a state of dependency and therefore appropriate for women? That is, if aging is a state of dependency, men should avoid it. In many of the jokes about aging there is a reason for the humor. It sometimes relieves anxieties. Many such jokes about aging are directed at the middle-age female. "Middle age is when a woman's youth changes from present tense to pretense. Thirty is the ideal age for a woman to be; particularly if she is forty. Time doesn't tell on women, it is their best friends who do." This tells you something about the model of aging that we have. Perhaps we have not changed our major opinions about aging in the last five years. If we haven't discarded an old idea or picked up a new one in all this time, we had better question ourselves.

Psychology looks at aging a little differently than does sociology or biology. I think there are four major ways that psychologists could look at aging. The first one is an impersonal one and deals with competence. Psychologists may regard a man or woman as an information system and ask what the information links with the environment are. That is, how much information can we receive and transmit per unit time? There is a fair amount of research that would suggest that we don't process as much information per unit time when we are older as we did when we were a young adult. Investigators at the University of Cambridge in England felt that they really could pin this down and estimate our information handling capacity as if it were the strength of a muscle or the capacity of a

*Director, Ethel Percy Andrus Gerontology Center, University of Southern California, Los Angeles.

communication channel. Their research addressed this question as though human processing was like figuring out how much information you can put over a telephone line. Their conclusion suggested that man can handle a finite number of information bits per second. This process involves receiving, translating, and decoding the bits of information and then sending a response back to the environment. It is something like the issue of how fast a stenographer can type. It appears that the bits processed per second diminish with age.

These findings conflict with other research which looks at changes in intellectual abilities with age. On some intellectual tasks there does seem to be a gain in capability with age. Particularly, there appears to be a continual increase in the amount of information that we have stored within us. All things being equal, if you have good health, you will continue to store information as you age. Your vocabulary is going to be significantly larger at age sixty-five than it was at forty, or even than it was when you graduated from college. Your vocabulary may double, in fact, over these years. As a college graduate you may have known 20,000 words and at sixty-five you may know over 40,000 words. This means that intellectual functioning, defined as stored information, is increasing as you age.

But, on the other hand, the information specialists are telling us that as one ages one searches that store of experience more slowly. Certain tasks and skills seem to be easier in early life than in late life. A quick response is a feat of youth. The more reasoned approach is an attribute of old age. Writing is a skill that flourishes in late life. If it is a skill that you can perform at your own rate and under no external pressure, you can maximize the value of stored information. On the other hand, if you have to respond quickly and on demand to certain stimuli, you are at a disadvantage in later life. Looking at this in terms of athletics, what sports show a maximization of skill at an early age, and what sports support excellence later in life? Golf involves skills of late maturity, because it is an athletic activity which you can do at your own rate. You don't hit the ball until you are ready for it. In other words, you can maximize experience. On the other hand, a boxer has to respond quickly to certain stimuli. He doesn't control the presentation of information. Boxing is apparently a skill that maximizes early so that boxers are "old" at thirty.

This suggests something about life. Having the opportunity to maximize on our experiences is what gives older people a sense of competence. The Cambridge research group studied occupations in some depth. They found that given a choice, men and women as they aged moved from jobs that put time pressure on them to jobs that were self-paced. So, to summarize this first psychological view of aging, time pressure is particularly em-

2

barrassing to older adults. It doesn't show them off to their best advantage. An understanding that this slowing is a normal part of aging might help older people get over their embarrassment about it. I don't feel particularly embarrassed if someone should tell me that I don't process as much information per unit time as I used to. This is no ego blow to me.

There is a concept I use to help me over any residual ego concern that may be involved in the fact that I am no longer as good an information processor. I explain the change using a conceptual approach. Let's go back to our processing model. If you have a secretary who puts letters in the file as they come in, you will have a complete chronological file, but one where it's difficult to have easy access to any one letter. So access time lengthens purely as a function of the amount stored. In our brains we take care of this filing problem by organizing information into a conceptural store. What were previously discrete bits of information now form a concept group. You reach through the concept to relevant experience. Let's take a practical example. We did interviewing at the University of Chicago of successful middle-aged men and women. One of the things they talked about is that they had come to deal with professional matters with less intensity in middle-age. A high school prinicpal said "When I started out, each disciplinary problem in the school was a special problem for me. I inter-vened; I went all out for it. Now I withdraw a little more and let the teacher handle it until I can see what is going on." As another example, the first-born child is a big crisis for the man and the woman. The first time the baby cries at home, the mother cries. There is much emotional involvement. This is not so with the second and third child. If only mothers could begin with their fourth child, then they could deal with the issues conceptually. With maturation comes a greater conceptual grasp so that we can size up the situation and then look to the relevant items in our store. This is what I call the race between the chunks and the bits. While younger people say, those between 18 and 22, can process more bits per second, and even though by age sixty that number may be halved, the older person may process bigger chunks. The race may go to the tortoise because he is chunking, and not to the hare because he is just bitting along.

There are, however, certain aspects of our society where time doesn't let us alone. I once spent some time observing people at street crossings in St. Petersburg, where a lot of older people live. Perhaps about thirty percent are over the age of sixty-five. We noticed that older people would only get to the middle of the street before the light turned red again. Some part of the available time had to be used for taking in information and recognizing that the signal had changed. It takes longer to

3

perceive the change from red to green when you are an older person. Also it takes a longer time to scan what is happening in the street, to see the approaching cars and estimate how fast they are coming, and to decide whether the cars will turn or not. So the older pedestrian scans carefully, and by the time he begins to move and steps off the curb a lot of time has already passed. Even stepping off a curb is a more time consuming task for the older person. He has to watch out for that too. The older adult has to monitor his physical movements more closely in order to avoid making a false move which might cause him to fall and injure himself. All of these concerns preoccupy the older person's attention. The result is that the step down into the street takes longer and these older people were able to get only to the middle of the street. What can we do? Will we adjust the cycle time of the stop lights to accommodate the older persons? That is a possibility. There is something obviously wrong if healthy people can get only to the middle of the street on the green light.

As we grow older we adapt to changes going on in our body. The way in which we handle problems changes. For example, if you find yourself in a situation where there are too many bits of information to handle, you experience a "cognitive overload." In order to deal with the situation, you are going to "load-shed." We all have devices for cognitive "load-shedding." The older pedestrian's way of load-shedding, their way of dealing with the cognitive overload experienced when crossing the street, was to cross following the lead of younger people. They would wait at the curb until some younger people were adjacent to them. Then they would simply follow the young people across the street. With this solution, the older people could make it across the street on the green light. The young people didn't know that they were being used to convoy the older people.

I want to emphasize that although the nervous system is changing, that change should not threaten us so much. I think there are other rewards. There are many ways for goodness to show itself other than in the number of bits or the frequency of firing of the neuron.

In England, P.M.A. Rabbitt has studied reaction to information displays as a function of their information content. It takes longer to deal with the display that has more information on it. Suppose I were to present a display of slides to you. One slide might be red and the other green. You have the choice to go if it is green, and to stop if red. You could make that decision fairly fast. But now I could present you with a three-choice situation, a four-choice or a five-choice situation. The speed of your response would be a direct function of the number of choices in the stimulus. This relationship works in

4

fairly lawful terms; that is, reaction time is a logarithmic function of the number of choices in the stimulus.

Rabbitt then went on to further study this relationship between stimulus complexity and response time. He incorporated not only relevant information in the stimulus display, but irrelevant information as well. Suppose we see projected on the screen not only red and/or green, but also other information such as letters of the alphabet. For example, directions might be given to raise your left hand if the number 1 appears on the screen but to raise your right hand when the number 2 is on the screen. The task gets more difficult if among the digits 1 and 2, are placed letters of the alphabet. You would begin to slow down because in this environment you must deal not only with relevant information, but also with irrelevant information. Also, Rabbitt discovered that older people slowed down more than the young people when there is irrelevant information in the environment. So, one reason why older people sometimes react more slowly may be that too much information is being processed. Older people are often dealing with too much irrelevant information along with the relevant, and cannot make choices rapidly. Is this distractability? Is it a function of attention? Is it a function of the fact that in the years since schooling we don't have to attend that closely any longer? I am not certain of the answers. I am pointing out that this is a phenomena of aging.

Not all changes with age are irreversible. This applies even to some of the physiological phenomena. Several investigators have shown that with increasing age the brain waves begin to slow down in frequency. Recordings from the scalp indicate that the dominant alpha frequency in young adults may be between ten and twelve cycles per second. The frequency may be seven and one half or eight cycles per second by age seventy. What is the significance of the dominant alpha slowing down? Surwillo maintains that reaction time relates to alpha frequency. He feels that one reason our response time is slow and our handling of information is slow when we are older is that this dominant alpha, this physiological pacemaker, is slowing down in frequency.

Diana Woodruff, a psychologist also persuing some of these issues, has been trying to modify this dominant alpha frequency with somatic feedback conditioning. By this technique, people can be conditioned to increase the percentage of time that their brain produces alpha waves. There is a whole area of research where we are just beginning to learn about somatic conditioning, and to investigate voluntary control of such functions as heart rate, blood pressure, or even peripheral circulation. Small rodents have been conditioned to cause a change of body temperature in response to stimuli. Woodruff

5

wanted to modify the frequency of brain waves. That is, she wanted to bring the brain waves of older persons up in frequency, and bring those of a young person down. She wanted to do this to see if it was possible to simulate older behavior in the young and younger behavior in the old. It turned out that by appropriate conditioning techniques she could modify the frequency of the brain wave. She could bring up the frequency in older people. Also, their reaction time did speed up somewhat, which gives us some evidence in support of Surwillo. However, this does not allow us to say that the whole issue is dispensed with by any means. The experiment on dominant alpha shows that there is some residual plasticity in the older nervous system, and not all of these changes are inevitable and irreparable. Under certain circumstances, the brain itself may even show some plasticity.

This is one way of looking at aging. Remember there are four or five different ways. This one we have just been talking about relies on the impersonal point of view. It assesses the competence of an older person without regard to whether you like or love him.

Another psychological point of view, also demanding a scientific approach, is behavior in relation to longevity. What relationships are there between the way we behave and how long we are going to live? In the January 1973 issue of the National Geographic there is an article by Dr. Alexander Leaf. He spent a sabbatical visiting three places in the world — the Caucasus, Kashmir, and Ecuador — places where people are reported to live disproportionately long lives. He found that it is true that these people do live a long time. Historical events, church records and other records verified the fact that these populations seemed to have a much greater proportion of the very old than we have in America.

It has been said that the reason there is a large proportion of older people in Russia is that no one really cares if they are old or not. There is more to it than that. Under the Czarist period in Russia, many men in the village took the same name. When the Czar's troups came through to draft men into the army, the village simply brought out the oldest man of all those with the same name. So longevity was an adaptive mechanism.

Leaf found that in the areas he visited there was a difference compared with our culture in the amount of activity people were involved in. All these long lived people come from a culture in which there is a lot of physical activity, also, their food intake was lower than ours, perhaps half of our caloric intake. There is another difference I think he missed because he is a physician. I am going to stress this social difference in my next way of looking at life span. (By the way, I want to say that when I read this article I was struck by a saying of one of the

6

old people that "every day is a gift when you are over 100", that each day is something special. I started to reflect about it and started to think this day is different for all of us too. It takes the older people to remind us that each day is really a gift.)

The next way of looking at the psychology of aging has to do with behavior in relation to disease and in particular to cardiovascular disease. What do research psychologists have to say about this? Two years ago in San Francisco, Freedman and Roseman identified a personality pattern intimately associated with the likelihood of developing cardiovascular disease. They called it the Type A personality. A Type A person is someone who feels time pressured, someone who assumes great responsibility. He is the all-American type, if you will, who works all hours, and has many diffused goals. When one task is finished, he runs to catch up with the next one. The studies that have been conducted suggest that these people are very prone to heart disease. A student of mine, Joel Abrahams did a study of civil service employees when they entered the civil service with regard to their physical examination, their physical status. He did a screening of these people and classified them as Type A or Type B. He found an interesting result. The Type A's showed behavioral slowing. Their reaction time was not fast, as you might think, but slow. In a sense, this looks like premature aging. These tense, hyper-active people, these rapid responders, are in fact slow responders. They cannot react to outside information as well as other people. They are always projecting themselves. They are slow to respond, and are not prone to receive information quickly and react to it. Perhaps we ought to begin identifying people with this behavioral pattern before they develop a coronary disease. Maybe there should be some kind of therapeutic intervention. What that would be at this stage I am not certain.

There is a relationship between the structure of the social environment and heart disease. This relationship is evident even in mouse communities. Dr. Henry of USC was able to produce hypertension and heart disease in mice as a function in the social environment in which they lived. If you raise mice in isolation and then form a colony with them in which they are forced to interact, they will never establish a stable, dominance-based social structure. The mice seem to be floundering and uncertain. They are always wondering who will go through the tube first to get the food. When these animals raised in isolation are put together in a social group, they are always biting each other. Their hair is ragged, they don't gain much weight, and they have a lot of scars around their tails from being bitten. The same strain of mice, when raised from birth in a colony which had a dominance structure, didn't argue and

7

didn't bite. These animals of same genetic strain did not show rises in blood pressure, or bio-cardio degeneration. This study shows that the social conditions under which animals live can result in hypertension and cardiovascular disease.

Different strains of mice react differently to the kind of environment structured around them. Some strains are so prone to hypertension and cardiovascular disease that given a small amount of encouragement by the environment, they show the trait. New Zealand mice are a strain very prone to cardiovascular problems; another strain is so phlegmatic that they bury themselves in the shavings, poke their noses up and let the traffic go by. So, there is a genetic potentiation and an environmental potentiation for susceptibility to cardiovascular disease and tension. I think that may also be the case with human populations.

Our style of life and our genetic make-up are factors influencing the way we age. Now we can refer back to those other cultures. I think what one sees in the Caucasus, Kashmir and Ecuador is a very stable culture where the relations with other people are highly predictable. You know the precedent. You may not like it, but you accept it. It seems that this stability of culture is better for somatic health. In our society, people struggle for their identity and struggle to get ahead. It might be better socially and psychologically to struggle, but it is going to have some physiological consequences. This applies to our society and our times. As women come in to the competitive arena of the marketplace after having led more subscribed lives, they are going to experience more of this ambiguity. We are certain to see rises in heart disease and in suicide in women in the next few years. The greater the ambiguity in our environment, the more the chronic stress, the more the disagreeable activity, the more we are going to see these diseases. Our environment is helping to potentate our genetic predisoposition to cardiovascular disease.

I have now given you four different points of view that psychologists use to describe the aging process. I have talked about the information model, longevity, disease predisposition, and social role. Our population in America is mobile and essentially is immigrant in its orientation. Ours is perhaps the most open of all societies. We are culturally heterogeneous; there are many ethnic substreams. This means that our relationships with other persons are not as predictable as they are in Sweden, for example, or in Holland. There is more religious homogeneity in both these countries which allows these people to feel some identity. However, look at the religious proliferation, the various countries of origin, and language backgrounds we have in our society. Not only do we move through social roles with age, but there is an ambiguity in our society as to

8

what roles are valuable. One person's role may be highly commendable in his eyes, but that role may be another person's anathema. There is no agreement in this open society as to what is admired and cherished. In fact, value issues are involved even in considering the activity or disengagement role for the aged. Is it good to be active with age? Or is it good to be sedentary? Should we become like the Greek men sitting in cafes and play dominos or cards and talk? Is that to be admired? There is uncertainty in our society about the appropriate way to behave. So much for social role.

There is a fifth way to look at aging, which is aging as it is experienced. How does it feel to be old? What does it look like to get old from the inside? This is different from the view of the experimental psychologist who wants to know how much information gets processed. As an individual, you are less interested in how much information than in what kind. What is it really like to be old? The answer to this question depends on where you are perceiving it from. At USC, one dissertation written in physical education had to do with leisure time activities of nursing home residents. This student interviewed nursing home residents and the staff members about desirable leisure time activity. An interesting thing came out of it. The staff judged the people as being less interested and less able to take advantage of leisure time activities than did the patients themselves. So, if I were a patient in a nursing home, and I wanted more activities and more contact with people, the staff member would be likely to say, "No, Jim Birren can't profit from all this, and he doesn't need it." Obviously there is a "perceptual gap" there.

I think this is partly an adaptive device on the part of the staff. If you put the patient down as not needing activity, then you don't have to feel guilty about not giving it. Some forgetfulness is not due to absent mindedness, but absent heartedness. I think we are sometimes guilty as professionals of assigning a certain image to a patient, which relieves us of feelings of responsibility.

We may like the life in an open society. We may be attracted to its options. But exercising options may be accompanied by tensions. You will live longer if you don't drink, don't smoke, quit gambling, stop chasing women, and stop staying up so late. (Of course, under those circumstances, even if one doesn't live longer, it will seem like longer!)

What are our models of aging? Who are our heros in growing older? The answer informs us about our directions for ourselves and what we implicitly want for our patients. What models of aging have you internalized?

The heroic model is a good one. Ethel Percy Andrus, for example, was her own person and a certain type of model. She

9

was a spinster, and when she retired after some forty years of teaching, she got $60.00 a month pension. This irritated her in her righteous way. She marched to the state legislature and convinced the people there that retired teachers should receive better pensions. Then she fought the battle of health insurance. At that time health insurance after age 65 was cancelled. She went to some thirty insurance companies and tried to convince them that they should underwrite insurance for older people. They wouldn't do it. Finally, on an experimental basis, one company did work out a policy and it has proved to be financially successful. Ethel Andrus, the heroic model. Is that the type of person we admire?

Or, do we admire the stoical person's adaptation to life? On a Christmas card I was sent the message: "Adapt to life and you will enjoy it." Is our model to be stoical? Is this the way to enjoy life?

Still another model is the angry model. It is one of protest: "That doctor really treated me poorly. I am going to sue him!" We know angry old people and we know angry young people. The angry young people grow up to be angry old people. Is that the style we want to internalize for our model? Angry people are getting some things done in society, there is no doubt about it. It is a very different model from the stoical, adaptive one. During the disturbances at Berkeley, a slogan was coined. "Never trust anyone over thirty." I wonder what the youths who enternalized that will be like when they are over 65? What kind of model for aging do these young people have? If they have really learned to hate older people that much, how are they going to face themselves at 65?

I am clearly describing to you personality types, but at the same time they are models of aging. There are other types, or models of aging. For example, there is the self-punishing type of older person: "If I had been smarter, I would have set aside more money and I wouldn't have to get along on this small pension." You will find many older people who have regrets. They are killing themselves with these regrets and this self-punishment. Another kind of person is the dependent type who simply will deny that anything is going on out there. This has consequences in certain stages of life. Jack Weinberg, a psychiatrist in Chicago, has spent a great deal of time treating middle-aged women who had grown up being physically attractive. These women had always been sought after. Then, one day, at a certain time of their life, the mirror on the wall no longer told them they were the most beautiful of all. You can defend yourself against this truth for a while, but eventually it gets to you. What do you do about it? Go to a psychiatrist? Men who have strong feelings about their bodies involving potency have a great deal of difficulty in middle-age if they have a coronary. Their egos are involved in their illness in such a way that they are very suicide-prone. Now this is a difference between the sexes. Physical being is terribly important to a man. So, when he loses some of his instrumentality, he thinks of himself very differently. He can't accept his own dependency. Women are used to being a little more dependent, so changes in physical being aren't as hard to accept. Physical illness and depression are closely linked in middle-aged men, especially in men who have a stereotyped view of masculinity.

Then there is what might be called the mature type. Here one tries to weigh the environment without attempting to box it up into black and white, good and bad, ups and downs, rights and wrongs. This person will try to estimate where he is with probabilities. He may have to adapt once in a while by being stoical, at other times by being angry, and once in a while by being heroic. In a population of people, the mature group is by no means the largest percentage. The studies at Berkely, done a few years ago, originally identified some of these types and they all apparently get along pretty well. Not only does a mature approach to aging produce life satisfaction, but even the dependent type can get along pretty well up until the point when his eggshell defense cracks. The passive, stoical, armchair types do reasonably well too.

I am suggesting to you that all of us have internalized a certain kind of model about aging. Some of these models don't leave us feeling particularly good about ourselves. What model do you have about aging? Be aware of it. It's certain that it affects your behavior and colors your experience of life.

II THE PSYCHOLOGY OF AGING

*Alexander Simon, M.D.**

In 1900, only three per cent of the population of the United States was age sixty-five or over. Today the figure is a little less than ten percent — about ten million women and eight million men. Around three-fourths of these men and less than half of the women are married; ninety-six percent live in the community; about twenty-six percent live alone or with non-relatives. Close to one-fourth of this population are living at poverty level or below. Unfortunately, many live considerably below poverty level. These poor, elderly persons live in large numbers in the deteriorated apartments, hotels, and rooming houses of the inner cities. They live close to Skid Row, and have to cope with alcoholics, drug addicts, and thieves in their daily struggle to maintain themselves. Afraid to walk on the streets, particularly at night, many exist in solitude and despair, fearful of dying unnoticed. Mental illness and social disability are serious problems in this age group, especially among those living in difficult social circumstances that may make it close to impossible for them to adapt to the inevitable physical and psychologic losses and stresses that come with aging.

Until eight or ten years ago, there was a general impression, even among psychiatrists who worked in state mental hospitals, that almost all old people who were incapacitated in any way were sent to mental hospitals because there was no other place for them to go. These old people were without families to care for them or else had families who wanted to "get rid" of them. In fact, however, only about five percent of the aged are in residential facilities of any kind, and only one percent are in mental hospitals. Nationally, only about thirty percent of the patients in state mental hospitals are over age sixty-five, even with the significant reduction in numbers of mental hospital patients of all ages that has taken place in recent years.

Hospitalized elderly mental patients fall into two groups. First, there are the patients who were admitted anywhere from ten to fifty years ago, most of whom are deteriorated schizophrenic patients who have grown old in the hospital. Second, there are the elderly patients who have been admitted for the first time after the age of sixty-five, most of them suffering from organic diseases of the brain (primarily senile brain disease or cerebral arteriosclerosis, and a small proportion

*Medical Director, Langley Porter Neuropsychiatric Institute, San Francisco, California.

from the so-called "presenile" brain disease.)

Of the elderly who are living in the community, about fifteen to twenty-five percent have moderate to severe psychiatric impairment. In some cases the impairment is as severe as that of elderly persons who have been hospitalized. During the 1960's, the Geriatric Research Project at Langley Porter carried out a large-scale study of the aged mentally ill in San Francisco. The study included a group of elderly patients admitted to the psychiatric wards of San Francisco General Hospital (many of whom were transferred to state mental hospitals) and a comparable sample (matched by age, sex, and whether or not they lived alone) who lived in the community. These two groups — 534 who were hospitalized and 600 living in the community — were studied over a period of two years. The hospitalized group was observed for an additional five to eight years. We found that sixteen percent of those living in the community were comparable in every way, even in severity of psychiatric impairment, to those who were sent to state mental hospitals. The only difference between the individuals in the two groups was that some were able to maintain themselves in the community where others could not. These findings are similar to those of ten or twelve studies that have been done in various parts of the world, mostly in Europe. They indicate that there are several million elderly persons in this country who are moderately or severely mentally ill, but who are not in institutions of any kind, and who need support and comprehensive care and are receiving practically none.

There are several reasons why some elderly community residents are able to stay out of hospitals despite often severe mental impairment. The most important reason is that, whatever their problems and disabilities, they are able to carry out those activities necessary to keep themselves functioning physically and socially, in however limited a way. Another reason is their very isolation. A good many simply do not come to the attention of caretakers such as police, physicians, nurses, social workers, or other agency personnel. Many older persons are isolated from community workers who might realize the need for hospitalization or other care and take some action that would result in removing the old person from the community into some kind of residential care facility. A third reason is that these elderly persons are much less physically ill than their counterparts who are in mental hospitals. This difference was strikingly demonstrated in our study by the mortality in the two groups over a two-year period. By the end of the first two years of the study, fifty percent of the hospitalized patients were dead, while only two percent of the moderately or severely psychiatrically impared community residents were dead.

What brings a patient to the point of hospitalization in the first place? There are two kinds of factors involved. Precipitating factors lead directly to the decision to seek hospitalization, whereas predisposing factors are believed to be casually related to the precipitating factors, but are not in themselves enough to force hospitalization. When we examined the reasons for admission among our hospitalized sample, we found they could be grouped into five general categories:

1. Disturbances in thinking and feeling, such as delusions and depression.
2. Physical illness.
3. Potentially harmful behavior, such as confusion or unmanageability.
4. Harmful behavior, such as refusing necessary medical care, or actual violence to others.
5. Environmental factors, such as the unavailability or incapacity of a responsible person to care for the patient.

Among the predisposing factors, disturbances of thinking and feeling, and physical illness were the most frequent. Among precipitating factors, potentially harmful behavior, and environmental factors were the most frequent. Predisposing factors could be present for a very long time, even for years. Families and others in the community could be quite tolerant of such things as depression, hallucinations, and even potentially harmful behavior, especially in very old persons. What finally precipitated hospitalization was most often potentially harmful behavior that led to a tremendous amount of anxiety on the part of the caretakers. In many cases, the precipitating factor was a change in the environment; a spouse died or someone who had cared for the patient could no longer do so. Some action had to be taken to provide needed care in an institutional setting instead. Actually, harmful behavior and physical health reasons were less frequently precepitants to hospitalization.

When a crisis situation makes placement of an elderly person necessary, how does he get to one kind of institution rather than another? Unfortunately, what determines where a patient is placed is not necessarily his condition and his needs. Where he is placed depends much more on what services happen to be available in his community, what their admission policies are, what the attitudes of the professional personnel are, who is going to pay and how much they can pay. Money, more than any other factor, may dictate the placement of elderly patients, even though we have known for a long time that if a patient is misplaced, (that is, if he is sent to an institution that does not meet his specific needs) he is more likely to die. For example, if a patient whose problem is primarily psychiatric is sent to a

15

general hospital or a patient whose problem is primarily physical is sent to a psychiatric hospital, he is more likely to die than is a patient who is sent to the kind of institution where the personnel are best able to deal with his particular needs.

Obviously, accurate and comprehensive evaluation and diagnosis are crucial so that the patient can be placed appropriately. During the past ten years or so, there has been a growing trend to screen patients both before they get to hospitals and after they are hospitalized (even after many years of hospitalization), with the goal of keeping them out of mental hospitals. Where do they go instead? It is said, euphemistically, that they are "discharged to the community." In fact, they go almost entirely to nursing homes, boarding homes, and sheltered care homes that serve as state hospitals in the community. So, under present conditions, these old people are being moved from one kind of "warehouse" to another kind of "warehouse." It is estimated that eighty percent of the residents of these homes are mentally impaired, and fifty percent of them are moderately to severely impaired. Because of the changing attitudes of caretaking personnel, there is a growing tolerance of aged patients who may be difficult to handle because of cognitive, emotional, or behavioral problems. But acceptance of such patients does not guarantee good care or even minimally adequate care. The problems associated with this trend toward alternative placement are causing increasing concern among responsible members of the health professions, the government, and the general public.

Studies of nursing homes, boarding homes, and sheltered care homes, where mentally ill, elderly patients live, have been conducted to determine the quality of placement procedures, follow-up procedures, and the actual services and resources available to the patients. The findings are quite discouraging. Referral documents from hospitals to the residential facilities are likely to be dreadfully inadequate. Almost none of them contains descriptions of the patient's behavior and level of function, special interests, particular behavior problems, or social habits that should be brought to the attention of caretaking personnel. There is sometimes a profound lack of interest in the placement process on the part of many of the professionals, including social workers and physicians. Professionals in the hospitals who are involved in the selection process often have inadequate information about the characteristics of available nursing and boarding homes. This makes it impossible for them to place patients appropriately. Follow-up is sporadic and inadequate. Boarding homes in particular may have inadequate outdoor recreation areas (or none at all), be poorly furnished and maintained, and rarely request psychiatric consultation. Similar deficiencies are found among nursing homes. When asked what additional services they would provide if more money were available, caretakers are likely to place psychiatric consultation low on their priority list. Few boarding homes and nursing homes can be considered adequate in all respects for the care of mentally disturbed or emotionally disturbed elderly patients, and I am sure this is true in all parts of the country. There are certainly nursing and boarding homes that do a reasonably good job despite the limitations imposed by lack of money and manpower. But these limitations make it inevitable that the elderly patients, who must depend upon such facilities in times of crisis or to provide a home during their final years, are deprived both of needed medical and psychiatric care. They are also deprived of the kind of surroundings and activities that can help them to feel like and to function as independent human beings, whatever their handicaps.

The needs of older persons are much like those of younger persons — to enjoy friendship and social contacts, to be busy at work and leisure activities in keeping with one's capacities, and to be in reasonably good health. Most people as they grow older are able to adapt more or less successfully to the changes that age brings in themselves and their lives. But the elderly are vulnerable to a number of stresses that include physical, psychologic, social, and economic deprivations. These stresses influence their physical and mental condition and their capacity for physical and social self-maintenance and self-sufficiency.

In general, we refer to the age period sixty-five and older as the period of senescence, without implying a deteriorating mental condition or any particular emotional problem. The term "senility" is used to describe an elderly person who does display definite symptoms of confusion, disorientation, and memory defect. For those who do show varying degrees of such changes, one can speak of "benign" or "malignant" senescence. "Benign senescence invoLes a mild but not especially socially disabling physical and mental deterioration, with slight memory defects. There is no frank disorientation or intellectual deterioration that interferes with day-to-day living activities. In such persons the deteriorative process, if present at all, progresses slowly and the individual is likely to live for years after he first subjectively observes such deficiencies or someone else objectively notices them. "Malignant" senescence refers to a senile process that is characterized by a fairly rapid and progressive deterioration over a period of months or several years. The deterioration is evidenced by an intellectual and physical decline in functional capacity. It is associated with a high probability of death within three or four years after the onset of overt symptoms.

The stresses to which the elderly are especially exposed include: physiologic stresses related to both decreased physical functional capacity and acute or chronic physical illness; psychologic stresses related to dependency, isolation, loneliness, and inter- and intrapersonal and intrafamily conflicts; and stresses arising from personal and socioeconomic losses such as retirement, widowhood, loss of family or friends, and loss of occupational status and adequate economic support.

We are generally aware that the bereaved constitute a high-risk group that must be offered help during the period of crisis. Retirement has profound implications for changes in an individual's social and economic status, in his interpersonal relationships, and in his self-perception and morale. It is not true, however, that many people die within a year or two after retirement as a result of the shock resulting from retirement itself. Those who die soon after retirement are usually those who retired because of health problems. Another kind of shock occurs when elderly people make drastic changes in their environment — a move from the Mid-West to Arizona or California, from a city apartment to a retirement community in an outlying area, or, for those who are living in institutions of one kind or another, a move from one home to another or from hospital to nursing home.

The significance of the direct relationship between poor physical health and psychiatric impairment is often overlooked. The elderly have a decreased physical capacity, loss of strength, vigor, and skill; an increased likelihood of chronic disabling disease; and an increased vulnerability to serious illnesses. It must be emphasized that physical health has been found to be more relevant to psychiatric impairment than any other factor. In our hospital sample, for example, eighty percent of the patients were suffering from physical illnesses serious enough to require supervision and health care. This has a tremendous public health significance. Although physical, social and economic factors are interrelated, if we did nothing more than improve the physical health of the aged by seeing to it that they receive routine, regular, comprehensive medical care, this service alone (even without improvement in economic status or social conditions) would do much to improve mental health and prevent problems serious enough to require hospitalization.

In the case of all these stressful situations, most of which represent losses of some kind (loss of spouse, loss of occupational status, loss of physical health, loss of family or friends) the older person may react in a number of ways. Some accept losses in a mature, realistic way. Some may react with a kind of overcompensation, a counterphobic attitude that may be within reasonably normal limits or may become psychopathologic. Examples of overcompensatory reactions are the older man who marries a very young girl as a reaction to waning potency, and the older person who gets caught up in excessive "physical culture" or food fads in an effort to build up his strength. These counterphobic reactions sometimes work, sometimes do not. Some persons react to stress and loss with a hypochondriacal reaction and develop all kinds of symptoms that permit a rationalization for the individual's waning ability to do things. Another reaction is to become angry with the environment, then to become depressed in reaction to the anger. Rationalization can occur at any age, of course, and does, because it explains away many of the problems people face. Another form that reaction may take is denial, the affirmation that the loss had not in fact taken place. This can lead to serious problems, especially when it involves the hiding of physical illness.

In conclusion, it must be emphasized that senility is not an inevitable aspect of the aging process, but is a psychologic, biologic, social, and cultural phenomenon that is modified by intrapersonal, extrapersonal, and interpersonal attitudes. It is fostered by many attitudes and actions toward the aged by individuals and by a youth-oriented society that has been described as gerontophobic. It is minimized by supporting and positive human activity and values and by appropriate consideration of individual differences and those derived from ethnic and minority group values. We tend to overgeneralize about a homogeneous group, defined by society as aged sixty-five and over. But the aged group sixty-five to seventy-five is different from that seventy-five and older. There are differences in health, social, and economic status, education, ethnic and cultural values, and between men and women.

For example, sexuality, instead of having a positive value of health and normality, as it does in younger persons, is often regarded as abnormal and "dirty" in older persons. Another prevailing attitude is to consider old persons "cute." This often occurs in hospitals and other institutions, where older patients are regarded as children, in a way that is insulting and patronizing. No matter how confused or regressed, the older person deserves to be treated with dignity. Another negative stereotype about aging relates to mental deterioration and memory loss. It is readily assumed by the older person who forgets a name or telephone number that he "must be getting old," whereas when a younger person forgets something, it is "something that can happen to anyone." In fact, the older person's memory lapse may be a function of underlying depression, such as can occur at any age. One of the professional stereotypes about memory is that remote memory in the aged is better than recent memory, although recent research has cast some doubt on this notion. When an older person is anxious to reminisce about his past, this may not be a function of a memory disturbance but rather that he takes greater pleasure in a pleasant reminiscence from his youth than in thoughts about the troubles, uncertainties, and problems of the present.

Many studies have shown that the better the education and the social and cultural background, the greater the resistance to mental impairment with age. But no matter what an individual's background, there is a pseudoimpairment that derives from apathy and a lack of meaningful personal relationships that may imitate dementia or chronic brain syndrome that does not in fact exist.

A further confirmation of the negative stereotype a number of physicians and other health care personnel have about old people is the reference to older persons as "old crocks." This expression of an underlying attitude is quickly picked up by medical and nursing students and carried by them and on to future generations for the rest of their lives. This point of view is expressed also in a fatalistic attitude about chronic disability. One notes it, too, in institutions of various kinds where the personnel tend to infantalize the aged patients by doing everything for them. As a result, the patients show what has been described as "excess disability," that is, a degree of disability that exceeds what could be expected on the basis of their real handicaps. When older people are in a nontherapeutic atmosphere, characterized by passivity, boredom, and day-to-day sameness, it is inevitable that a seeming disorientation will occur. Persons in such an atmosphere will respond to questions about orientation with "I don't know," when they really mean "I don't give a damn!"

It must be emphasized that all institutions are not bad for old people, only the custodial, nontherapeutic institutions are. Robert Butler and Erik Erikson have, in different ways, emphasized that older people tend to go through a life review process as they age in an effort to understand the meaning of their lives, their interpersonal relationships and accomplishments. This tendency to self-awareness can be used to good purpose to help them to live their remaining days with a fuller understanding and acceptance of their abilities and disabilities.

III   MENTAL HEALTH IN THE AGED

Irene Mortneson Burnside, R.N., M.S.

In James Kavanaugh's book, *There Are Men Too Gentle to Live Among Wolves*, is a poem entitled, "Old Man." The last part of the poem goes like this:

"Damn the life that took me from you!
Damn the world that keeps you alive
And shoves you aside.
Damn me for forgetting you in the agony
    of present pain.
I love you old man, feeble old man
With rumpled hat,
Fighting old man who will struggle
    Fiercely 'till the day he dies.
Not paranoia this, as learned doctors diagnose —
Only a tired old man who has
    lost the sophisticated pretense
    that obscured your lonely
    struggle and locked it wordlessly
    in your heart!"[1]

Although the poet mentions the mental condition, paranoia, I am not going to dwell on that. Instead, I am going to talk about the lonely struggles of the aged. Not too long ago, I met with a Senior Citizen's group in Los Angeles, and I asked this group of elderly people what they thought the mental health problems of the aged were. These were their answers delivered without hesitation:

1. Loneliness
2. Depression
3. Brain damage
4. The meaninglessness of their lives

In this paper, I would like to narrow the broad field of mental health of the aged to these four rather simply stated components of mental health, and share with you some of my ideas and clinical experience. If we are going to have any impact on the bleak lives of many old people, I think we have to acknowledge the problems they express to us, and begin there. I guess I learned that from a wise old patient who finally convinced me that Copenhagen snuff was better for him than aueromycin, and also cheaper. This same old man taught me

Coordinator for Nursing Education, Ethel Percy Andrus Gerontology Center, University of Southern California.

how well old people can problem solve, if we only listen to them and allow them a chance to try their own strategies. For example, Mr. C. was in a nursing home; he was blind, and in a wheel chair. He was 84 years old, and had a third grade education. He loved ginger snaps and kept a large bag of them on his bedside table. Since he was blind, he often could not tell when people were helping themselves to his cookies. He said the worst offenders were the night staff, and since he slept soundly, the cookie-snatching was getting worse. He had a friend buy a mouse trap for him, then every night, he set the mouse trap and placed it in the cookie bag. Of course, it worked.

LONELINESS

There is an increasing amount of material being written on loneliness. Loneliness is a human condition, but I want to focus only on loneliness in the aged. I once had a student describe behavior in the elderly in this way:

"The behavior pattern that frustrates me the most is the clinging to you — the terrible loneliness — the feeling that no one cares anymore — that this is the end of the road."

We find loneliness, depression, mental changes, and the expression that life is meaningless in aged persons everywhere. These problems exist for institutionalized elderly, for the elderly living at home, and for those in the geriatric ghettos, the run-down hotels in the inner cities. Busse says of institutionalized patients:

". . . the states of mind in which the fact that there were people in one's past life is more or less forgotten, and the hope that there may be interpersonal relationships in one's future life is out of the realm of expectation or imagination."

This definition applies particularly to the aged because it seems to me that many of them have little ego energy left to invest in new relationships to replace those they have lost. Perhaps you have heard people say that it is harder to make friends as one gets older. Because friendships for the aged dwindle, the grocer, milkman, or paper boy, become the people who are important to them.[4] I have known mail carriers and milkmen who have kept a close eye on some of the frail elderly on their route.

One of the classic articles on loneliness in the aged is by Clark Moustakas. In the article, "Communal Loneliness," Moustakas describes therapy with a seventy-four year old man. At the last session, the gentleman said, "I came only to see your face light up, to be warmed by the gleam in your eyes. I know how much you suffered. I have seen your tortured face even after leaving you. I'll sit here with you quietly a few minutes."[5]

Eloise Clark has developed a framework for nursing intervention on aspects of loneliness.6 She spells out the steps — the increase in anxiety, the increase in the degree of loneliness, and states that defenses such as denial, suppression, repression, alcoholism, and somatic complaints are defenses used by an individual to decrease feelings of anxiety and also to diminish the pain of loneliness. Three themes emerge from her work. One is that loneliness is a part of man's humanity. Another is that defenses are often used as protections from the pain of loneliness. The third is that loneliness is felt in degrees ranging from mild to profound. She suggests that the inability to love may also be related to the degree that loneliness is experienced. She concludes, "A nurse ... must provide a relationship in which there is an openness to involvement."7 I do not think we nurses have a corner on such involvement; a multitude of persons need to be involved with the aged to decrease loneliness. In that multitude I believe there should be babies, children, and adolescents, and even pets.

The poet gives us advice about the intervening with a lonely, depressed person:

"Let me not terrify you with closeness,
Nor alienate you with barren chasms of distance."8

These are simple sentences, but not so easy to implement if you've tried working with lonely people.

DEPRESSION

Depressed states, like loneliness, are of varying degrees and are frequently seen in the middle aged and elderly. I have included the middle aged here because we really do need to consider the problems of the middle aged people.

Stanley Cath has written about the "basic anchorages" we need in our lives. He states that these anchorages are crucial to us:

1. an intact body and body image
2. an acceptable home
3. a socio-economic anchorage
4. a meaningful identity and purpose to life9

He further states that during a depressive phase ". . . circumstances sometimes conspire so that nothing of value for substitution is available or acceptable."10

The losses often are health losses, especially sensory losses. Loss of sight, loss of hearing, loss of limbs or other body parts, for instance the loss of a breast in women, contributes to depressions and concern about body image. Old people managing colostomies must certainly deal with a drastic change in body image.

The changes which occur in aging have been described so beautifully by John Steinbeck in *East of Eden*. The children arrive home for a holiday. The parents go to bed and the grown children remain and discuss their aged father:

"They all wanted to say the same thing — all ten of them. Samuel was an old man. It was as startling a discovery as the sudden seeing of a ghost. Somehow they had believed it couldn't happen. They drank their whiskey and talked softly of the new thought.

His shoulders — did you see how they slump? And there's no spring in his step.

His toes drag a little, but it's not that — it's in his eyes. His eyes are old.

He never would go to bed until last.

Did you notice he forgot what he was saying right in the middle of a story?

It's his skin told me. It's gone wrinkled, and the backs of his hands have turned transparent.

He favors his right leg.

Yes, but that's the one the horse broke.

I know, but he never favored it before.

They said these things in outrage. This can't happen, they were saying. Father can't be an old man. Samuel is young as the dawn — the perpetual dawn.

He might get old as midday maybe, but sweet God! The evening cannot come, and the night—? Sweet God, no!"

Body image is often neglected in psychosocial nursing care. I like what Jean Kerr wrote, "I'm tired of all this nonsense about beauty being skin-deep — that's deep enough. What do you want, an adorable pancreas?"[11]

The loss of loved ones is a steady irreplaceable loss for the aged, and Busse describes the loss of spouse as "the most grievous assault of all."[12]

Last summer, Groucho Marx was interviewed for a newspaper story. I clipped it out because he captured so much about aging in a few terse sentences: The newspaper reporter wrote that Groucho often gets lonely for his brothers, Harpo, Chico, and Zeppo — all now dead.

"They're gone, and as you'll find out when you're older, it gets sad . . . I've seen it all here, you know. When you're my age, you have. You've seen it all, you've got nothing to lose, and you've got nothing to be terrified about."[13]

APATHY: A MASKED DEPRESSION?

Apathy is a term commonly used to describe a state that is often a masked depression in the aged.[14] I have observed that the apathy of the institutionalized aged is more drastic than the aged persons I have seen who are still living at home. As a professional, I find that it is sad to watch the gradual decline of an aged client into a state of apathy. Think how difficult and painful it must be for the family to view such deterioration.

I once did home nursing and my case load included a tiny little woman who wanted to be called Rosa. She was Italian; her husband was dead. I saw her daily (and often on weekends) to give her insulin, for she was a rather severe diabetic. We had coffee every morning I was there. She was very frugal and saved on dishes and dishwashing by using an egg carton for her breakfast plate. However, she always served me coffee in her best china. Sometimes when she made cioppini she insisted I taste it or take a cup of it with me for my lunch. Rosa taught me a lot about the aging process. About being poor. ("Da testa tubes they cost 14 centa piece — lotza money for so little glass.") About not being able to see well, about living in a deteriorating neighborhood in a deteriorating house, and being afraid to answer the door. About loneliness. About depression. And she also taught me about apathy.

Maintaining her in her own home was a tenuous situation, and one day after I left the case, she was admitted to a nursing home. Another nurse and I went to visit her. We were appalled at her downhill condition. The apathy was there with a capital "A". She no longer cared about her garden or if the prickly pear cacti were in bloom, or cioppini, or making coffee. She had given up; her losses seemed to have defeated her.

In my office, I have what I call a LOSS and FOUND box. LOSS, that is, and not lost. L-O-S-S. I keep ideas for substituting for losses in the aged in this box. We need to consider some of the ordinary everyday items and materials used. For example, how about a giant-sized deck of cards that can be used for the visually impaired? You can buy an ordinary sized deck with enlarged numerals on the cards. You can also buy a geriatric exercise record which can be done with patients sitting in wheel chairs. A little transistor radio should be required for all elderly blind people to help them stay in contact with reality. We also need to look at the canes, the crutches, all the accoutrements of aging — are they the best ones for that person? Perhaps they need to be replaced. A more suitable cane? Adjusted crutches? Stronger glasses? Stronger light bulbs in the reading lamps? Bigger clocks and calendars?

Gramlich listens to somatic complaints in the aged, which may be helping to mask depression. He suggests telling old people why they are hurting, and that they are grieving, for he states that often they do not associate the pain of the grief with the loss they have suffered.[15]

We need to consider interventions which help to increase the self-esteem of the many depressed, withdrawn aged individuals. We also need to assist the aged with substitutions for the losses they have experienced. Can we afford to let them be shoved aside? We need many disciplines working together on the losses of the aged, losses which can lead to depression and even to suicide sometimes.

CHRONIC BRAIN SYNDROME

I am using the term brain damage, because that is how the elderly woman described it that day in Santa Monica, but I am going to talk about chronic brain syndrome, which Robert Butler has called a "waste basket diagnosis." Wang states that:

"Any impairment of the brain tissue is usually accompanied by impairment of those cognitive functions that are directly dependent on the activity of the brain tissue involved. Disorientation, memory loss, impairment of intellectual function and judgment are therefore considered the primary characteristics of organic brain syndromes."[16]

We need to distinguish acute confusional states from chronic confusional states. An acute syndrome is temporary and the state is thought to be reversible. When the syndrome is irreversible and considered to be permanent, it is called chronic brain syndrome.[17]

Let me share with you some of my clinical experience with six chronic brain syndrome patients of a locked psychiatric facility in California. I have six elderly patients, three men and three women, all with the diagnosis of chronic brain syndrome. The mean age is 77. Two walk fairly well, one shuffles, two are in wheel chairs. Three persons in the group can write their names. Two speak coherently most of the time. Two are fairly coherent but slow on the uptake. Two do not speak verbally, but they can speak fluently non-verbally!

My initial objectives in working with these six were: (1) to increase stimuli for these patients to see if their level of response or coherence could be changed, (2) to reality test consistently, (3) to use food as an adjunct to therapy. The last objective fell by the wayside after the first meeting. I discovered after listing the objectives that these patients were on a five meal per day feeding. On the day when I could be at the facility and meet with them, they were scheduled to eat right after our meeting. So that objective was out. During the first meeting, I wondered where to begin, since I had felt the need of a constant theme to use with these persons each meeting to provide structure.

I went around the circle and shook hands with each person and held their hand awhile and tried to maintain close, intense, eye contact with them. I came to the last frail little lady in the group who weighs 85 pounds. She was babbling, had her eyes closed, and I suddenly doubted my ability to do much of anything with this group of persons. I took her small, fragile hand with tissue paper skin and seemingly crushable bones in her hand. She reminded me of this Japanese poem:

"I picked up my mother
In play, but when I
lifted that frail light body
I was so overcome
I could not take three steps."[18]

As I held her hand lightly, she took her other arm and put it around my neck and kissed me tenderly on the cheek. All behavior has meaning. She was communicating regardless of her babbling and disorientation. Her behavior subsequently then influenced my behavior with the group. She was the best example of "touch hunger" I had seen in a long while. I decided then to use much touching each time I was with them. I had planned to count each time I touched them, but I would forget and spontaneously reach out to a member. I also found myself touching the blind man more frequently to explain things to him, and increase his reality because he was hallucinating. I told him he would have to talk to God on his own time, because when I was there, he had to interact with me. One man had been coaxed off the top of a building in Los Angeles by the police last year when he was 85. Because I had read his words on the chart to the police, "What's the use of living?" I am sure that I touched him more often also.

I do increase the times I touch them each visit. My tactics are not scientific, but they are working, and do bear out for me what Harry Stack Sullivan said about loneliness, ". . . we have an inborn desire to touch one another and to be physically close — beyond the closeness of the sexual embrace per se."[19] Ruth McCorkle did her thesis on "Touch in Seriously-Ill Patients," which reinforced my ideas about the importance of touch.[20]

As I go on with this group, I find that past experiences with schizophrenic patients in my psychiatric nursing are helpful with the group in these ways: (1) the leader needs to constantly reality test, (2) the leader needs to be patient, consistent and provide structure, (3) the leader needs to have the ability to tolerate silence, muteness, hallucinating, and babbling, (4) and to be able to continually study non-verbal communication.

A good example of non-verbal behavior occurred in the fifth meeting of the group. I almost missed my chair when I sat down, and the two most regressed members of the group had been watching me and laughed at me. I was delighted to see them smile for the first time, even at my expense.

Mr. K's comment to the police, "What's the use of living?" leads me to the fourth category, meaninglessness.

MEANINGLESSNESS

I find that the topic of meaninglessness is the most difficult of these four to grapple with, so perhaps that is why I have left it until the very last. Some years ago, when I was in graduate school, Dr. Paul Tournier, the Swiss psychiatrist, came to this country to speak. He told about a young girl in therapy with him who had a complete psychotic break and he had diagnosed her as a schizophrenic. In therapy one day, Dr. Tournier told her he was going to the United States to speak and asked her what she would like to have him tell the people there. The young girl thought for a long time and then soberly replied, "Tell them that they must find meaning in their life."[19] Her words came back to haunt me when I was in Santa Monica, and the elderly people there told me about the meaninglessness of their lives.

Do you remember this in *Future Shock* by Alvin Toffler? "One winter night, I witnessed a poignant quiver run through a seminar room when a white-haired man explained to a group of strangers what had brought him there to attend my class on The Sociology of the Future. The group included corporate long-range planners, staff from major foundations, publishers and research centers. Each participant spieled off his reason for attending. Finally, it was the turn of the little man in the corner. He spoke in cracked, but eloquent English: 'My name is Charles Stein. I am a needle worker all my life. I am seventy-seven years old, and I want to get what I didn't get in my youth. I want to know about the future. I want to die an educated man!'"[21]

In group work with the aged, one often hears the aged ruefully state their lack of education. I wonder what we can do to start classes geared to the learning needs of the elderly people. They are asking for meaningful work and ideas and thoughts too.

One of the things that we frequently do in nursing homes is to assign meaningless tasks to the residents who may still have some wherewithal and then wonder why they are not happy about doing them. I recall one instance in which a woman crocheted long strings of chain stitches. Then the nurse came in and took them all away and took them to another patient to unravel and to roll into balls of thread to later be taken back and crocheted all over again. Or we give them stuffed animals or dolls to love and hug like we would give tiny children. Or we wonder why a poker-playing former truck driver does not like to play bingo. Or a concert music lover hates making pot holders. If lives are already meaningless and the aged tell us this, then why do we reinforce it by activities that could seem demeaning to the aged individual? Jung has said, "The

28

afternoon of life can't be lived with the rules of morning."[22]

I would like to pose some possible approaches to intervening in loneliness, depression, brain damage, and meaninglessness.

1. We'll have to ask the aged what for them are meaningful thoughts, activities, people and objects.
2. We need to help elderly people find compensations and substitutions for their multiple losses.
3. We need to share and listen. Why not tape their stories? Why not records of achievements? We do not have any.
4. We need more studies like the one by Strauss and Glaser, a case history entitled, *Anguish*.[24] That study is the death trajectory of a middle-aged woman with cancer, but what about case studies on the aged?
5. How are we going to increase and improve treatment modalities? What about more one-to-one relationships with elderly, what about more groups of all descriptions, at all levels, in a variety of settings? Ebersole has done some pioneering work using reminiscing as a focus in groups of aged hospitalized persons.[25] What about family therapy with aged families? Why not place student nurses in Senior Centers to help with the physical and mental problems that the ambulatory aged have?
6. What about the use and misuse of drugs in the elderly? What drugs or combination of drugs are causing side effects — perhaps confusion, or depression which compound existing problems?
7. And let's not forget to study successful aging!

I began with poetry and I would like to end with poetry. This excerpt is from Edna St. Vincent Millay:

"Life must go on — I forget just why."

I think we can begin to change that for aged people if we really try. Don't you?

REFERENCES

1. Kavanaugh, James. *There Are Men Too Gentle to Live Among Wolves,* Nash Publishing, Los Angeles, 1970.
2. Busse, Ewald W., and Eric Pfeiffer. "Functional Psychiatric Disorders in Old Age," in *Behavior and Adaptation in Late Life,* (ed.) Ewald W. Busse and Eric Pfeiffer. Little, Brown, and Co., Boston, 1969, p. 188.
3. Fromm Reichmann, Frieda. "On Loneliness," in *Psychoanalysis and Psychotherapy,* (ed.) H.M. Bullock, University of Chicago Press, Chicago, 1959, p. 327.
4. Streib, Gordon. "Micro-Environments and the Well-Being of the Aged." Paper presented at International Congress of Gerontology, Kiev, U.S.S.R., July 7, 1972.
5. Moustakas, Clark. "Communal Loneliness," *Psychologica,* 1960, 3, p. 190.
6. Clark Eloise. *Developing Behavioral Concepts in Nursing,* (ed.) Loretta T. Ziderad, Helen C. Belcher, Southern Regional Board, Atlanta, Georgia, 1968, p. 40.
7. *Ibid.,* p. 40.
8. Santopietro, Mary-Charles. "Wishes for a Lonely, Depressed Patient," *Perspectives in Psychiatric Care,* Vol. X, No. 3, 1972, p. 139.
9. Cath, Stanley H. "Depletion and Restitution," in *Geriatric Psychiatry,* (ed.) Martin A. Berezin and Stanley H. Cath, International Universities Press, Inc., New York, 1965, p. 188.
10. *Ibid,* p. 33.
11. *Wisdom of Women,* (ed.) Canada Jessup, Random House, 1971, p. 31.
12. Op. Cit., Busse et. al., p. 188.
13. *San Francisco Examiner,* July 24, 1971, p. 32.
14. Levin, Sidney, "Depression in the Aged," in *Geriatric Psychiatry,* (ed.) Martin A. Berezin and Stanley H. Cath, International Universities Press, Inc., New York, 1965, p. 205.
15. *Gramlich, Edwin P. "Recognition and Management of Grief in Elderly* Patients," *Geriatrics,* July, 1968.
16. Wang, H. Shan. "Organic Brain Syndromes," in *Behavior Adaptations in Late Life,* (ed.) Busse and Pfeiffer, Little, Brown, and Co., Boston, 1969, p. 267.
17. *Ibid,* p. 267.
18. Source unknown.
19. "Schools of Psychoanalytic Thought," (ed.) Ruth Monre, Holt, Rinehart, Winston, New York, 1955, p. 360.
20. McCorkle, Ruth. "Touch in Seriously-Ill Patients," Unpublishes thesis.
21. Toffler, Alvin. *Future Shock,* Bantam Books, Inc., New York, 1970, pp. 426-427.
22. Jung, Carl. *The Structure and Dynamics of the Psyche,* Trans. by R.F.C. Hull, Bollingen Series XX, Pantheon Books, New York, 1960.
23. *Ibid,* Cath.
24. Strauss, Anselm L., and Barney G. Glaser, *Anguish: A Case History of a Dying Trajectory,* The Sociology Press, Mill Valley, California, 1970.
25. Ebersole, Priscilla. "Reminiscent Group Therapy for the Aged," Unpublished manuscript.

IV   THE PHYSIOLOGY OF AGING

*Caleb Finch, Ph.D.**

Each individual human being seems to have a slightly different pattern of aging from any other human being. This fact makes it very difficult to establish the causes of aging. Taking a comparative view, related animal species seem to have a common manner of aging. Of course, there are some basic similarities among mammals, but fish and insects are very different. Perhaps the best point of departure in the discussion of what physiological aging consists of would be a glance at a mortality curve. The structure of a number of human populations by age is shown in Figure 1.

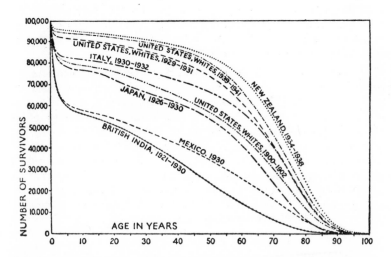

Figure 1. Survival curves for various human populations. (From Comfort. 1956. The Biology of Senescence. Holt, Rinehart, and Winston, Inc., New York.)

The top curve shows the survival rate in New Zealand. These people had a very long lifespan in the 1930's, perhaps even longer than the average lifespan in the United States today. For New Zealanders, there is very little mortality up to about the age of fifty. Then mortality increases sharply, setting a

Professor of Biology and Gerontology, University of Southern California.

maximum lifespan somewhere around 100, and an average lifespan at about seventy-five. Looking at the bottom curve, a very different situation is apparent. This is the curve for British India in the 1920's, when there was tremendous epidemic of infectious disease and malnutrition. High infant mortality is reflected in the left-hand portion of the curve which then declines and rises again to yield an average mortality at about thirty-five years. But again, the maximum lifespan isn't that different from New Zealand. Our general conclusion is that environmental factors influence average lifespan, but don't influence the maximum longevity.

At the gerontology laboratory run by the National Institute of Health in Baltimore, the eminent physiologist Nathan Shock is conducting a number of studies on the physiological changes of aging. He has been observing people of various ages and has been testing heart functions under a number of experimental conditions including mild exercise. Perhaps the most significant finding is that there are highly predictable changes in the ability of the human body to withstand stress. This may be one of the more prominent hallmarks of change during aging in any population. This change seems to be independent of diet and of many of the other disease variables.

To understand aging, it is necessary to understand the major causes of death. There is really quite a broad spectrum of causes. We know that each human group typically has different causes of death. Heart disease predominates in some populations, and cancer or tuberculosis in others. Tuberculosis, for instance, is now declining as a cause of death for the aged. If one examines small laboratory rodents, which are often used as models for aging because they go through their lifespan in a shorter period of time, the same diversity of diseases can be seen. There are some strains which die of mammary cancer; there are others which die of kidney disease, and still others die of anemia.

There are many measures of how stress is less tolerated in the aging organism. One of them, which I used experimentally, is the ability to maintain body temperature during cold exposure. Old people often complain about being cold or uncomfortable at a room temperature which many others of younger age find perfectly comfortable. There is a counterpart of this phenomena in the laboratory mouse.

In Figure 2, the internal temperatures of (young) ten months old mice and old mice that are thirty months old are shown. When these mice were put into a forty-five degree Fahrenheit environment for three hours, the younger mice maintained their

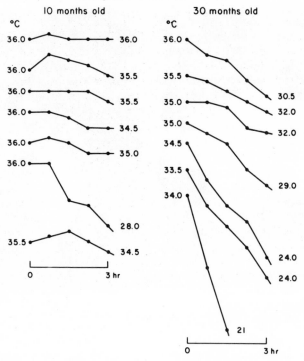

Individual Records of Colon Temperature
during Cold Stress (9–10°C)

Figure 2.   Individual records of colon temperature during cold stress (9-10ºC) in young and old mice. (From Finch, et al. 1969. Gen. Physiol. 54: 697.)

temperature perfectly well, but the older ones suffered intense drops of body temperatures. This is a clear experimental demonstration which lends support to the common feeling of cold that many humans experience during aging. It is rather remarkable that we find the same change in that same portion of the lifespan of a mouse. Because so many of these human stress changes can be observed in mice and rats, this gives us some confidence in studying rodents as models of human aging.

To emphasize again the diversity of changes during aging and how much these changes can be affected by the environment, Figure 3 shows a rat on the left which appears withered, old, and close to death. The rat on the other side appears plump, vigorous and young. These rats were actually the same age. The one on the left was fed on a high fat diet all its life. It has become badly wasted during aging and suffers here the terminal effects of the diseases of aging. These diseases have probably been influenced by the diet. The rat on the right was always fed less than it wanted to eat. This rat is in the pink of health.

Figure 3.   This photo shows that diet has a visible effect on the processes of aging. (From McCay. 1952. Cowdry's Problems of Aging. A.I. Lansing [Ed.]).

These two animals were from the same litter; they were brothers. It is possible to see from an experimental point of view the great importance of environmental variables.

This photograph of the rats dramatizes the tremendous difficulty presented the biologist trying to understand the fundamental changes of aging. One of the changes that I have begun to study because of its universality is the phenomenon of menopause. Despite the great differences in disease patterns for human populations and in the course of aging, in all human women between the ages of forty and fifty there is the phenomenon of menopause, the cessation of menstruation. This is probably one of the most definite landmarks of aging in human women. Although there can be really remarkable differences between the ages of forty and sixty in the physical appearance and general health of women, the end of the reproductive age occurs at about the same time in all women. It also commonly occurs in the same period of the lifespan (halfway through) in laboratory rats and mice. Menopause is probably one of these phenomena that can definitely be called an aging change. It is a change which is not the result of a bad diet, or some other hazard from the environment.

The phenomenon of menopause can be analyzed in a rather fascinating way. I would like to present a short biological analysis of what menopause is, of why women have it, of what the consequences are, and how these consequences might possibly be avoided. I should say at the outset that there is no phenomenon corresponding to menopause in men. There is no time after puberty in males, either human or rat, when the male is infertile or incapable of the reproductive act. This is, of course, contrary to the general myth about men.

When menstruation ceases at menopause, the reproduction system is no longer capable of bringing the fertilized egg to full development. This may correspond to the increase of birth defects in children of women over forty years old. The phenomenon of menstruation, which involves the stripping off of a layer of the uterus once a month, is really controlled by the ovary which sends out a regularly scheduled pulse of hormones to bring about changes throughout the body. It is obvious that much more than the uterus is affected by that regular monthly cycle of hormone secretion.

It is logical to ask what the ovaries are doing at the time of menopause. It is well established that the ovaries stop producing over 90% of their secretion of hormones. This is a major and tremendous loss in hormone production. It is, at the present time, the best documented example of hormone changes during aging in humans. This change is indicated in Figure 4. The dotted line on the top represents the estrogen levels in normal women. The small bars on the bottom line represent the estrogen levels in post-menopausal women. You can see that there is a terrific loss of estrogen. As compared to women who have had their ovaries removed for surgical reasons, shown by the bar in the lower right-hand corner, you can see that the ovary is almost as nonfunctional as far as making hormones after menopause. The women without ovaries act as a biological control to verify this analysis of hormones before and after menopause. By taking the ovary out to see what is still produced, it is possible to see that women without ovaries produce just about the same amount of estrogen as the women after menopause. This change in hormone production, which is not found in men, has a tremendous number of consequences in a woman's body. All those tissues and organs which change at puberty, now deprived of hormones, undergo regression.

One of the major questions biologists are asking at present is how many of the phenomena of aging in human women are the result of this loss of hormones? We know that hormone production changes in the ovaries at the time of menopause. Knowing this, we must ask another question. Why are they producing less hormones? We know that the ovaries are controlled by another organ at the base of the brain called the pituitary. The ovary is not an independent system, it receives its signal from other endocrine glands in the brain which regulate

35

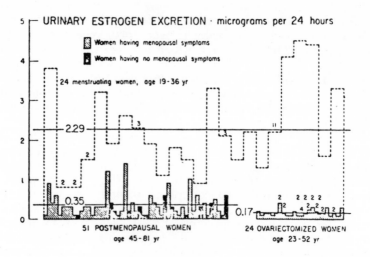

Figure 4. Data on the normally menstruating, post menopausal and ovariectromized patients are arranged along the abcissa from left to right, according to increasing age, years after the menopause, and time since castration, respectively. When more than one observation was made per patient, the bar indicates the average and the digits above the bar represent the total number of observations. (From Paulsen, et al. 1958. J. Am., Ger. Soc. 6: 805.)

its activity. The question is, does the ovary age because of an intrinsic change within it, or does it age because of a change in the signals to it from the brain and the pituitary? This question could be answered by transplanting the ovary from an old female rat after its equivalent of menopause to a young rat. This experiment has been done by Ascheim and Krohn: it is quite clear that the ovary, after reproduction has ceased, is still capable of normal cycles if the old ovary is transplanted to a young body. The young rats continued to menstruate. The old ovaries were still capable of producing normal eggs which, when fertilized, grew to become young normal rats. Although the ovary in the body stops making its hormones during aging, it still has the capacity to respond to those signals originated elsewhere in the body which regulate the hormones. This is a fascinating experiment because it suggests that in at least some cells in the body in natural aging, changes are not intrinsic to these cells but are the result of signals from elsewhere in the body.

Let us now examine a few of the consequences of the loss of estrogens which do appear to be widespread. These consequences are avoidable if the estrogens and various hormones are replaced. One of the more common causes of invalidism in older women is their great tendency to develop fractures of the hip or other bones. In some women, the bone becomes so weak and soft that it cannot support their bodies even under normal circumstances. This is a clinical condition known as osteoporosis, meaning reabsorption of the bone. In many women with osteoporosis, there is a very dramatic loss of height; the spine of these women actually decreases in length. Figure 5 is an

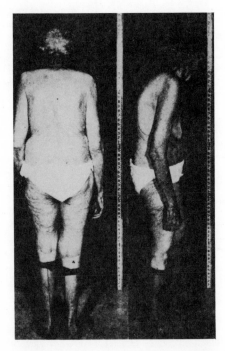

Figure 5.   I.C. photograph of a 79-year old woman, under observation and treatment for a period of 10 years, for pathologic osteoporosis and periodic episodes of vertebral collapse, fractures and 1-1/2 inch measurement of loss in height. (From Urist, Gurvey, and Fareed. 1970. Osteoporosis. U.S. Barzel [Ed.]. Grune and Stratton, Inc. New York.)

illustration taken from a clinical journal as an acute form of this loss of bone in the spine. The spine has become so weak that it has begun to collapse. You can see the curvature in the photograph. Women with an acute form of this normal aging condition do indeed become shorter. In fact, this disease, as an exaggerated age change, progresses until the margin of the ribs comes to rest on the bone of the hip and the body structure is supported again. This change in its acute form is an exaggeration of the normal change which occurs during aging and is apparently the result of loss of estrogen made by the ovaries.

As early as the late 1940's it was known that in the process of aging estrogens stop being produced by the body. Figure 6

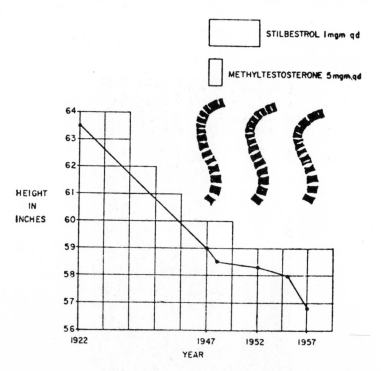

Figure 6.   Summary of height and roentgenographic findings in 69-year old woman with post menopausal osteoporosis. Patient received estrogen therapy from 1947 to 1952. Height loss and vertebral compression resumed after discontinuation of therapy. (From Wallach and Henneman. 1959. J. Am. Assn. 171: 1640.)

shows the height chart for a woman who after menopause developed a very acute loss of height. This woman was given replacements from 1947 to 1956. You can see that during this period of time her height loss was arrested. But then because of complications and problems in the hormone treatment, it became necessary to stop giving her the hormones. The loss of height began again. This indicates that height change is under the control of hormones which, when given to replace the loss of hormones during aging, arrest the change. When five years later the hormones were removed, the change began again. In general, there is an observable loss of height before estrogen therapy, and an arrest in the loss of height once estrogen is given. So it is quite clear that for many women suffering from this kind of change in their skeletons, the change can be arrested by the simple replacement of the hormones which the ovaries no longer make.

It wouldn't be fair if I gave a general encouraging note that all aging changes in women could be arrested by taking hormones. It is quite clear that there are many which cannot. Nevertheless, there are many studies under way right now to investigate how these hormones could affect some of the diseases of women which appear after menopause. One of the diseases which usually has been considered a problem of the male is that of heart disease. It is well known that after menopause, there is a big increase in coronary heart disease in women. The incidence of coronary heart disease for women in their sixties approaches that in men of the same age. This is a ten or twenty-fold increase in heart disease in women in a ten-year period. We know that the major physiological event that happens in this ten-year period is the cessation of the ovary producing hormones. A large project in New York City (Rockefeller University, Cornell University Medical College, and the College of Physicians and Surgeons of Columbia University) is studying the effect of giving hormones to women on the incidence of heart disease. There are a number of reasons to suspect that the replacement of estrogen will greatly reduce the incidence of heart disease in women after menopause. Many cellular changes are probably directly related to this loss of estrogen. This loss is really very great, and extends far beyond the sexual organs. This loss effects the uterus and vagina, and probably affects many other organ systems including the bones, the blood vessels, and quite possibly the skin. At present, very little concrete, definite information is available. Nevertheless, it is clear that replacement of some hormones, in some women, has a tremendously beneficial effect. In the next ten or fifteen years of research, the picture will become much clearer, because it is now beginning to be studied in a thorough way. The tragic caricature of an elderly woman, hunched over, with tufts of hair coming out of her chin, and unable to move comfortably, may be an unnecessary predicament, and, with the right doses of hormones, may be entirely avoidable. I don't wish to give the impression that all aging in women can be arrested by a simple replacement of hormones, but a number of changes, such as acute loss of bone can be controlled. This will, of course, offer a tremendous possibility for a greater length of vitality to women in their 60's, 70's and 80's. In the near future, we may see a totally new profile of what aging is and of what the expectations of growing older in women are. The social implications are terrific.

I have stated that the ovary does not receive its signals internally, but that it is under the control of another part of the body. In the brain, the master hormones go out from the pituitary to the thyroid and adrenal glands and the ovary to instruct them on the level of their activity. Recall the experiment in which an ovary of an old mouse was transplanted to a young mouse: the old ovary was capable of normal function. This indicates that aging in the ovary is under the control of some other part of the body. A rather fascinating experiment is being done now at Michigan State University in the endocrinology lab of Joseph Meites and his colleagues. He has shown that by implanting an electrode in that part of the brain of an old rat which controls the endocrine system, the hypothalamus, it is possible by just a little electric stimulation, only a few thousandths of a volt, to reactivate the ovary. Research in the physiology of aging is quite analogous to an auto mechanic testing an engine which won't start. In this case, the ovary could be "jump-started" by stimulation of the brain. This is remarkable because it suggests that a large number of changes resulting from the ovary's function may actually result from changes in a very small region in the brain. In other words, there may be pacemakers of aging in certain parts of the body which regulate the course of aging throughout the rest of the body. Our research is directed toward this possibility. We are studying how aging affects those parts of the brain. There is a tiny part of the brain, called the hypothalamus, which regulates the pituitary. What we have found is that there are some very definite chemical changes in the nerve cells of aging mice. In fact, the metabolism, the activity of nerve cells, is much smaller in the old mouse. This is demonstrated in Figure 7. This figure shows what physiologists call the turnover or rate of production of molecules which are concerned with the electrical activity of the brain cells. These molecules, related to adrenalin, are called nerve transmitters. They connect the activities of two nerve cells and are very important in the control of hormones. Figure 11 also shows the turnover or lifespan of these molecules in young mice and in old mice. There is a tremendous difference in the rate of metabolism of these nerve transmitters in the young and old mice. This may be direct physical evidence that there

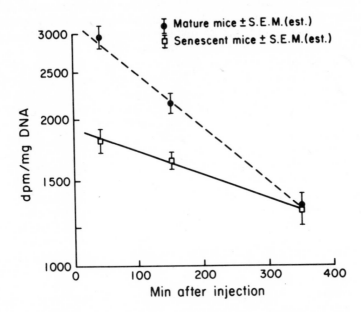

³H-Norepinephrine Turnover in Hypothalamus
(³H-l-dopa precursor)

Mature mice ± S.E.M.(est.)
Senescent mice ± S.E.M.(est.)

Figure 7.   Turnover of hypothalamic norephinephrine ([3H] NE). (From Finch. 1973. Brain Research. 52:269.)

are primary changes of aging in the brain. We are, of course, investigating the nature of these changes very intensively, hoping to find out what controls their aging and what their consequences are in terms of function of the brain.

In summation, it looks as though there are some phenomena of aging which are under the control of hormones. Some of these phenomena, like menopause, seem to occur universally in all human populations. Therefore, these changes can really be called natural changes of aging and are not the result of bad diet, infectous disease, or cigarette smoking. We are trying to identify what the general changes of aging are and to learn how many of these changes result from alteration of hormones. In at least one case, the changes in women after menopause, many of these changes are result of a loss of the hormones of the ovaries and can be in part compensated for by supplying estrogen to make up what the ovary has stopped producing. Although these changes may be under the control of the brain, I do not envisage a society of the future consisting of people over forty walking around with electrodes in their brain. When the biologists suggest that certain hormones may be replaced to prevent some of the more disastrous consequences of aging, I think they are doing no more than suggesting a modern refinement of the use of animal skin by our caveman ancestors to protect the body from the ravages of nature. The idea behind our research is nothing grotesque, but is simply to extend our knowledge of the aging and to improve life.

V   CHANGING PHYSIOLOGY OF AGING

*Ruth B. Weg, Ph.D.**

AGING AND THE SEARCH FOR PROLONGEVITY

All people, administrators, clergy, dieticians, nurses, social workers, teachers, students, researchers, practitioners in every area — young, middle aged and older; men and women are together in a world in which time and change are among the most critical of realities. It seems appropriate in the aftermath of the 9th International Congress of Gerontology at Kiev in July of 1972 that a brief comment by the Russian philosopher, Nikolai Berdyaev, (1874-1948) be recalled. He describes how the old man would "plead passionately for the insignificance and unreality of time, and then suddenly stop and look at his watch with genuine anxiety at the thought that he was two minutes late for taking his medicine."

It is also appropriate to bring you to the way of life for many old people in contemporary society. The only character is an old woman, fiercely alive. She is dressed in a white, rumpled hospital gown and carries her life inside a paper shopping bag. Her conversation is addressed to the figure of Death who appears to her as various men: her husband, her father, the dentist, a moving man. The audience, however, sees no one except the old woman. A description and two stanzas of a poem tell the story. She speaks:

"I'd die before I ever let myself get old.
I would always stay young.
And what did I want for my life to be?
I wanted then
the same as I want now:
everything!
To go everywhere in the world,
to be everybody in the world,
to slide under the ocean — climb over the moon
swing back and forth between them
thumbing my nose."**

And why not? All through the ages, the human family has clutched at youth, and when old, has sought all manner of means to recapture youth and live long lives. In the literature of ancient Greece and Rome, the philosophers, orators, poets, essayists, biologists, are always described as "people of years."

Associate Professor of Biology, Department of Biology, Associate Director for Training.
**From a poem "A Conversation against Death" by Eve Merriam.*

Epimenides of Crete (poet and philosopher, 7th century B.C.) lived to be 153 — and it was said, "he was son of a nymph." Democritus (460 B.C.), Zeno (4-3 century B.C.), Thales of Miletus (640-546 B.C.), all were described to be about 100. To Aristotle, who wrote "On Longevity" "On Yough and Age" "On Life and Death," old age was inevitable, natural — to be accepted.

Cicero (1st century B.C.), in his essay on senescence argued that, "it is not old age that is at fault, but rather our attitude towards it." Hippocrates, Xenophon, Cicero, Seneca, Plutarch, Galen — and others all wrote about "aging great men," and each of them had special prescriptions for long life as well. It was Galen, a Greek physician of the 2nd century, who, combining much of Greco-Roman medical thought of that day, described aging as "beginning at the very moment of conception." He concurred with Aristotle, that "Aging is not a disease, because it is not contrary to nature."[1]

Written in the old Testament is Isaiah's vision of "new heaven and new earth — where men will live so long that one who dies at age of 100 will be considered a mere child." The value of long life is built into Christian writings. In Ecclesiastes, the prolongation of life is promised as reward for righteousness. In Genesis (6:3) "man . . . also is flesh; yet his days shall be a hundred and twenty years."

Sexually based vitality has been a major concept throughout the ages as well. Vitality was thought to be inherent in young males. Many therapies, ancient and modern, and prescriptions for youth and longevity are thus related to sexuality.[2] The Taoist philosophers of the East (350-250 B.C.) developed highly detailed respiratory, dietary, gymnastic, spiritual and sexual techniques in order to conserve and support the body "essence" or semen. Preparations with a base of tigers' testes appear in many old Chinese pharmacopeoias; and van der Bossche was prescribing the genitalia of a cock in 1638. Brown-Sequard, at the end of the 19th century, concluded that aging is due to the gradual loss of sexual activity, and tested injections of testicular extract on himself. He announced his findings to the Societé de Biologie de Paris in 1889 and his colleagues responded with satire. Sergé Voronov in the 1920's experimented with testicular fragments from anthropoid apes, and his method of testicular grafting made him famous in the years that followed World War I. Yet, we know today that most transplants are rejected. His apparent success may have been related to the well known placebo effect. If we look for benefit from all this experimentation, these genital matter compounds may best be viewed as the logical previews to the understanding of hormones — their sources and uses. Real knowledge did accumulate from all the experimentation.

From antiquity through today, many have advised restraint of sexual activity. The suggested frequency of sexual activity optimum for health and long life is as varied as the number of advisors. Some have advocated, e.g. Montaigne and Buffon in the 18th century, that "the body use all its energies, that it consume all it is able to consume, and that it exercise itself as much as possible." In Yoga — restriction is favored, related to mystic ideas about vital energy. With others, it is a question of holding onto, or using up gradually, given amounts of energy. This energy used up too quickly would leave little for later life. Many have held that asceticism leads to long life. There is indeed evidence that a monastic life style, characterized by asceticism, does seem to correlate with great age. It is written in Ecclesiasticus (37:31): "By surfeiting have many perished; but he that taketh heed prolongeth his life."

Many body systems or processes that exhibit changes with time at one point or another, have been hailed as the trigger for all of aging processes. Buffon (French naturalist, 1707-1788) tried to explain the earlier death of men as compared with women on the basis of a belief that found slerotic disease (hardening of organs and tissues) to be the cause for aging. He said, "As bones, cartilage, muscles and all other parts of the body are less solid and softer in women than in men, so more time is necessary in order that these parts may acquire that hardness which causes death. Consequently women need more aging than men ... Once past a certain age, women live longer than men." Lumiere, a French chemist of the 19th/20th century, concluded that flocculation of cellular colloids, together with dehydration, contributed to old age. Still others pointed to changes in the nervous system, and some to changes in the metabolic rate. Metchnikoff (naturalist, bacteriologist, 1845-1916) believed that intestinal autointoxication brought on aging, and advised ingestion of special bacilli to counteract toxins and regain youth. This still goes on today in many "health farms," where high colonics are used to refaunate and reflorate the intestinal tract.

And what of magic potions and the alchemists' elixirs? "Essence of Viper" and "Viper's water" as the source of rejuvenation was mentioned by Pliny in the first century A.D. The belief in their efficacy probably arose in India, where it was thought that people who ate vipers lived to be 400 years old. The alchemists of the Middle Ages made a mixture called the "elixir of life," a tincture of the Philosopher's Stone (an imaginary stone or chemical preparation with power to transmute base metals). Raymond Lully, Spanish philosopher of the 13th century, wrote in *The Illuminated Doctor*, of a drinkable gold suitable for reviving centenarians, but failed to include the formula. Francis Bacon (1561-1626) offered remedies: use of gold, pearls, precious gems, amber and bezoars, not to mention the heartbone of a deer — the hardened root of the aorta of an old deer.[1]

There have been in past times "Fountains of Youth," according to legend established by Jupiter, the Roman god, the "light bringer," whose consort, Juno, used the waters at Canathos. As we move into our own lifetimes, perhaps from the 1950's on, magic and youth quest are ever present in similar and different guises:

1. Dr. Saint Pierre in France, who claims you are as old as your blood, injects blood serum into older men and women. How modern is this? Herophilus, before the 1st century A.D. (even before Pliny the Elder, a scholar 23-79 A.D.), and author Celsus the Younger, 62-113 A.D., mentioned hemotherapeutics as used by the Egyptians.
2. The late Dr. Paul Niehans of Switzerland, used injections of cells of unborn lambs into human beings to restore health and vitality. It is conceivable there may be some positive effects, such as enzyme induction or increased hormonal activity and the proliferation of embryonic cells.
3. What of the claim of Dr. Robert A. Wilson, gynecologist, who wrote *Feminine Forever*, that the rate of aging could be slowed with estrogen replacement?
4. There is Ivan Popov's aromatotherapy in France, for which some people have paid up to $25,000 for the privilege of smelling certain perfumes.
5. What of Dr. Ana Aslan's procaine and vitamin therapy? Since 1951, she has claimed that injections of what was called KH3 will retard or reverse aging. She also suggests that Gerovital (its current name) provides the patient with increased resources to fight a host of other conditions (deafness, poor vision, impotence, heart disease, ulcer, hypertension, arthritis.) Recently, the Federal Drug Administration has approved some limited research on Gerovital, primarily in relation to connective tissue disease and the sedation effect of the drug.

PHYSIOLOGICAL CHANGES WITH TIME

What are the realities of changing physiology with time as far as we can know them today, almost into the 21st century? Most of all, we know that not all the functional changes we see in older people are due to aging; some are pathological; some due to disuse. We know that there are great individual differences in rates of aging, and in the way people age. We know that age changes over the period of time between twenty and sixty years in the same individual are gradual when studied over time. Different organ systems in the same person age at different rates. Under resting conditions, some physiological parameters change very little with age; these measurements in the old are comparable with the young.[3]

We also know what we see: The bright eyes are less so, some grayed with cataracts. The tall grow shorter, the nape of the neck more round. They who ran, choose to walk; knees may bend, but not so deeply. The skin gathers brown, so-called "liver spots"; wrinkles appear where once there were laugh lines. And the crown of glory is not so glorious; the hair is thinner, grayer.

What more have we learned: [4, 5]

1. In general, there is a steady decline in functional capacities with time in cells, tissues, organs, systems and therefore the whole person.

2. Perhaps the most significant alteration is with the integration function of the nervous system in its role as coordinator of the interactions of muscles, glands, neurons and blood. This could account for the easily observable changes over time in the locomotor system; muscle tone and strength appear to peak between twenty and thirty years, and then decline. Conduction of nerve impulse decreases in the elderly. This represents, however, only a ten to fifteen percent loss as compared with the young. Simple neurological function remains relatively unimpaired. But acts of everyday living, e.g. walking, getting up, lifting, bathing, cooking, are made up of many nerve to gland, nerve to muscle, and nerve to nerve connections. And so loss in conduction rate (probably related to activities at the synapse) is compounded. Long bone and vertebrae density also decreases, and more recently, biochemical changes in muscle and cartilage are being measured. However, measurements of separate components of the locomotor system muscular, neural, glandular, and circulatory do not add up to the apparent overall loss of speed, flexibility, reserve and coordination. Thus, the decrease in integrative function of the nervous system is viewed as critical.

3. There are often signs of malnutrition: loss of appetite generally coupled to loss of teeth, ill fitting dentures, decreases in senses of smell, taste and vision. If this is compounded with a decrease in flow of digestive juices, reduction in peristalsis, increased constipation, and a good deal of "sweets eating," even the effect of a well balanced diet is minimized.

47

4. All the senses decrease in sensitivity with time, not only smell, taste and vision, but touch and audition. Losses in audition, primarily at higher frequencies, which begin at adolescence, appear to peak between forty and fifty years.
5. With increasing age, there is also a measurable reduction in the efficiency of the breathing mechanism. This is characterized by decreases in maximum breathing capacity, residual lung volume, vital capacity, and basal O_2 consumption. Since energy and the raw materials for being and growing are derived from O_2 combining with nutrients, the older individual may generally have decreased reserves, and therefore, more difficulty with health maintenance.
6. We have found that the cardiovascular function also shows change with time. Cardiac output and stroke index go down; the heart works harder to achieve less. Renal blood flow, glomerular filration and tubular excretion rates decrease — there is an estimate of 55% decrease of blood plasma flow through kidneys between the ages of three to eighty. However, peripheral resistance, circulation time and systolic blood pressure increase in many older persons. This is especially so in those individuals whose blood vessels have narrowed with atherosclerosis and arteriosclerosis.
7. One of the most striking differences between young and old can be seen in response to stress, a decrease in capacity to readjust to change, to return to equilibrium. Certain parameters, such as blood sugar, blood proteins, pH, blood volume, even heart rate and blood pressure are relatively stable and not very different in young and old subjects at rest. However, such an observation may tell us little about real capacity. With stress, whether physical as in exercise, or emotional in excitement or fear, the magnitude of displacement is greater, and the rate of recovery is slower with increasing age — thus homeostasis is less easily maintained in older persons. This changing capacity for stress response can be identified by the decrease of certain hormones in urinary excretion. One of the first measurable hormonal responses to stress is ACTH, the trophic hormone of the anterior pituitary; this in turn stimulates the adrenal cortex to secrete the corticoids. Another measure of body response to stress is an initial rise in urine level of adrenaline and noradrenaline secreted by the adrenal medulla.
8. Other hormonal responses are known to decline with age.[6] Hormones favoring immunity processes decrease, e.g. thyroxine, thyrotropic hormone from the pituitary and

the thymus hormone. This last is probably more important than has been earlier supposed, since it appears to stimulate the proliferation of those cells that synthesize the immune bodies or antibodies. On the other hand, there is an increase in the autoimmune response. It has been suggested that faulty antibodies may be synthesized, and as such remain attached to cells and lead to the destruction of healthy tissues. Or, possible DNA (gene) change or RNA and enzymatic alteration may produce cells and tissues that are recognized as non-self, and are destroyed by normal antibodies. Gonadal hormones also decrease over time in men and women. This decline produces slow, involutionary genital tissue changes. In post-menopausal women, there is gradual atrophy of vaginal tissues, marked by low levels of lubrication; the uterus and cervix also decrease in size. In men, the steady decrease in testosterone is accompanied by lowered rate of spermatogenesis, decrease in viable sperm, and frequent difficulty in achieving and maintaining erection. It is true, therefore, that there are changes in sexuality with age, but not incompetence. Sexual performance is less frequent, and not as predictable as in earlier years.

CELLULAR AND MOLECULAR BASES OF CHANGES

How can we explain these changes? In the same way we seek to explain function at any age, by looking to the cells and the molecules that make up the human body. All that has been provided up to now is descriptive and, in the main, gross physiological modifications with time. But not all cells and tissues of the body age in the same way, nor can they be characterized as the same in general behavior. Some cells of the body retain the ability to reproduce all through life, e.g. skin, lining of the gut, liver and bone marrow cells (blood cell producers). This capacity for regeneration does, however, appear to slow down with age. Some cells lose the capacity for mitosis before birth or shortly thereafter, e.g. neurons, muscle cells, kidney cells. Death of these cells leaves the body with fewer functional units. It is possible this process of regular loss without replacement could go to a point of less than minimal body mass that is necessary to maintain life, and so death of the whole person results.

The third material, connective tissue, is non-cellular and is the major component between cells. This intercellular substance, which also lines blood vessels, made up of collagen and elastin fibers, changes with time and contributes to structural and functional alterations in major blood vessels and large organ systems. Fibers become less soluble, less elastic, and are thought

49

to diminish intercellular exchange.7, 8

Some explanations therefore, may be developed for those systemic changes mentioned earlier. It may be then that in systems whose cells still have the capacity to divide, that the slowed rate of repair accompanied by any somatic, chromosomal errors, could result in dysfunctional enzymes or faulty structural proteins. This, in turn, interferes with liver function, with hormonal levels, and therefore many cell processes. What of those systems whose cells no longer have the regenerative ability? An irreplaceable loss of these cells, and decreased efficiency of those that remain, could underlie some of the described changes in function of the brain, heart, other muscles and kidney. There is no doubt that the older brain has fewer neurons (loses up to 100 grams or 10% or less of total brain). Senile plaques (made up of tangles of neurofibrils, glial cells and mucoploysaccharides), which render that portion of the brain dysfunctional may increase. The kidney has fewer nephrons with an estimated 8% decrement per year after the age of thirty. Skeletal muscle is obviously lost with age. Aging pigment, lipofuscin, appears to increase in brain, heart, and skeletal muscle. More cellular membranes are fragmented. Nuclei and mitochondria are fewer and show marked atypia. Trace metals, Ca^{++}, K^+, Na^+, among others, are noticeably out of balance in tissues, blood and urine of older persons.

Is this all there is; is aging a gradual decline in function?[3,4,5] There are those who add, what of disease? What of the pathology that appears to be part of aging. What are the facts?

1. morbidity and mortality do go up with age
2. increased incidence and severity of the 3 major chronic diseases — cardiovascular, cancer and stroke are beyond question
3. emphysema, rheumatism, arthritis, and broken bones are also more widespread in the old and have been most neglected by medicine and the biomedical revolution to date.
4. these pathologies do often exist in the last one-half to one-fourth of life, and the bulk of deaths from these diseases are among the old
5. age and disease are indeed frequently coincident. Yet no cause and effect has been established between disease and age, merely statistical evidence of increased susceptibility to disease.

CHANGE AS THE DYNAMIC IN HEALTH AND DISEASE
It is my particular belief that disease is not an inevitable partner of our older years. If age is not the primary contributing factor to the widespread pathology that characterizes older

people, what is? Recent studies have accumulated some evidence that suggests that life change alone may be one of the more important gerontological factors. Death of a spouse, marriage, retirement, divorce, residential move, job change, enough of these in one year, could lead to serious illness. There is a reported 75% correlation between the number of life change units on a "Social Readjustment Rating Scale," and the seriousness of illness. This scale has been applied to a wide variety of groups — unemployed black people in Watts, naval officers at sea, people in the United States, Japan, France, Belgium and the Netherlands. The correlation between the number of life changes and illness held; the higher the number of life changes, the more serious the illness. Similar patterns were found among pregnant women, leukemic patient families, and retirees. There was a highly significant correlation between life change scores and chronic disease — (leukemia, cancer, heart attack, schizophrenia, menstrual difficulties and warts.)[9] It is a short step from these studies to the realization that the aged in contemporary society experience great changes: loss of status, loss of jobs, decrease in income, loss of friends and relatives, change in living arrangements; and often loss in level of former physical capacities. It is apparent that all of these changes from a prior, more advantageous state produce stress and may tax the individual's coping abilities to the limit, leading to a breakdown of adaptability and disease.

Thus far, the physiology has been isolated to be examined more carefully; however, the social setting and emotional load cannot be separated from the working body. All of these interact in the whole human being, as the studies with life change appear to indicate. Ample independent evidence is available to substantiate the notion that frank pathology may result when provoked by psycho-social stress. In one experiment, thirty-one Army officers took part in a seventy-five hour session at an electronic shooting range without sleep, relaxation or stimulants. Sedimentation rate increased 168%; serum Fe went down 52%; protein bound iodine (for thyroxine) increased 30%; adrenaline reached maximum levels, and 25% of the subjects developed pathological electrocardiograms suggesting infarction.

Another example of emotion translated into biochemical changes leading to physiological dysfunction can be found in the human digestive tract. Response to fright and depression is marked by hypofunction — nausea, vomiting. Response to aggressive attitudes of anger and resentment is hyperfunction. If frustration and repressed conflict are sustained, the fragility of the gastric mucosa membrane is increased, small erosions develop, and bleeding points increase to become the bleeding ulcer of a competitive, industrialized society.

NORMAL AGING: PRESENT AND PROMISE

What are the possibilities for normal aging without pathology? Promise for the future is all around us. Conclusions of two recent studies by independent researchers, Chebotarev in the Soviet Union, and Palmore in the U.S., identified four common predictors for increased longevity that include: maintain a positive view of life, maintain good physical function, and avoid smoking.[10, 11a, 11b.] Opportunities for workers in the function, and avoid smoking. Opportunities for workers in the field of aging, and in fact for all people, suggest themselves to help validate these data.

In the week from February 12-16, 1973, the Andrus Gerontology Center at the University of Southern California was dedicated with a convocation of scholars and 550 NRTA/AARP visitors from all over the country. Among the scholars were Eric Hoffer, self-taught philosopher and former longshoreman; Nathan Shock, eminent research gerontologist, and Gregor Piatigorsky, the great cellist. All are over sixty, and two in the seventh decade. All are vigorous, healthy, involved, formidable human beings. Piatigorsky shared warming, gentle thoughts as he began, "After all, we all know that good wine tastes best, as old fiddles sound best."

Instances of new creativity in old continue to mount.[12] Michaelangelo was chipping away at sculpture a few weeks before death in his ninetieth year. Titian was still painting at 99 when he was cut down by the plague. Verdi wrote "Falstaff" at 80. Tolstoy wrote "What is Art" at 88. Freud, who predicted his premature death at 42, at 61 and again at 81½, died at 83. Though he himself was pessimistic about the creativity of the aged, and about the degree to which the older person could be helped, he wrote "The Ego and the Id" at 67.

Further examples of creativity and production into the late, late years include: Grandma Moses, the elderly Primitive painter. Santayana, a philosopher, who wrote his first novel, *The Last Puritan,* at 72. Sherrington, the physiologist turned philosopher, wrote "Man on His Nature" in his old age. Pearl Buck, the author, recently died in her 80's. Pablo Casals, the cellist of world reknown, is still playing and in his 90's. Pablo Picasso, the painter and ceramist of many moods and phenomenal talent, was still at work in his 90's, died at 91. Few of these people have been the beneficiaries of the biomedical revolution.

With society's victory over infectious diseases and infant mortality in the past century, is it unreasonable to anticipate that the next 25 years will find the major diseases accompanying old age all but eliminated? They represent the next frontier in the achievement of health as the World Health Organization defines it, "a state of complete physical, mental and social well being" — not merely the absence of disease or infirmity.

There is promise indeed represented in the long-lived peoples of the world: in the Andean village of Vilcabamba in Ecuador, the land of the Hunza in the Karakoram Range in Kashmir, and in Abkhasia in the Georgian Soviet Republic, Southern Soviet Union. As a matter of fact, those who have lived the longest seem to be those remote from medical practice, as well as other aspects of modern civilization.

Professor G.E. Pitzkhelauri, head of the gerontological center in Tbilisi, Georgia, identifies three major sources for validated information about age of the long lived peoples. The first level of records include church baptismal records, birth records, passports, letters, writings, carvings on doors and walls. For the second level of corroborating evidence, he has used age at marriage, time until birth of children, present ages of these offspring. On the third level, although not as precise, and not in writing, supporting data has been found in memories of outstanding events, war service, change in czarist regimes, the Russian revolution, and so on. As an example, Muslimov, a Russian peasant of Azberbaijan, said to be 165, is still at work, has never been ill, and is able to recall incidents of 150 years ago. There may even be some inaccuracies, some exaggeration in the claims of little or no coronary disease, no mental illness, no stroke or cancer among the Abkhasians. However, Dr. Alexander Leaf of the Harvard School of Medicine and Dr. Sula Benet, an anthropologist from Hunter College, have spent the past few years visiting these people and studying. They find this phenomenal lack of pathology among these people who indeed are aged, wrinkled and vigorous. [13], [14], [15] It would appear there are pockets of normal aging in all parts of the world. It may remain for investigators to tease out of the "all alike," "all decrepit" myth that weighs heavily on cultural attitudes the great variety of individual life styles, the different ways to grow old without disease.

Does this mean that the data about decline in function with age as described is being ignored? Diminution of some capacities are measurable, even in healthy, older persons. What is significant however, is that the remaining capacities are more than sufficient in millions of older persons. A satisfying physical, mental and emotional life is possible for the majority of older persons if the society finds value in providing a reasonable framework.

Are these losses with age subject to control, to retardation? Here are some answers to that question:

1. Muscle strength and tone can be regained with an exercise regime of six to eight weeks for 60-90 year old men, and

for older women as well.[16]

2. Changes in diet, protein and vitamin therapy are able to reverse some confusion, fatigue, irritability, insomnia and even so-called "senility."[17]

3. Osteoporosis, so often mentioned as typical or "normal" in post-menopausal women, may also be a syndrome not due primarily to age changes, but to a lifetime of faulty diet and hormonal imbalance. There is every reason to believe this loss of calcium from the skeleton can be modified with attention to diet and general health throughout the life cycle.[18]

4. The loss of teeth, and periodontal disease so marked in the elderly are not inevitable. Prevention, again in the earlier years, will keep the destructive processes to a minimum, maintaining optimum jaw and soft oral tissue relationships for a longer period.

5. If an attractive eating situation is provided to a human being who happens to be old and alone, then appetites improve, energy levels go up, and susceptibility to disease goes down.

6. Masters and Johnson have demonstrated that healthy sexual activity may continue into the eighth and ninth decades. All that is needed is an "interested and interesting partner," and some patient reeducation.[19]

It would seem then, that an important percentage of the diminished function may be due to society's attitudes, disuse, misuse, lack of information, rather than solely a function of age.

Longitudinal studies in various research centers in the world give further promise for the reality of normal aging. Dr. Nathan Shock, in a presentation at the Andrus Gerontology Center in February, 1973, spoke about preliminary analyses with data from a study of age changes in 600 males between twenty and ninety-six, begun in 1958. This study at the Gerontology Research Center in Baltimore includes biochemical, physiological and psychological tests. Results indicate that functional changes with time in the same individual are not nearly as marked as in individual subjects from cross sectional curves used in much aging literature.

In laboratories studying aging processes all over the world, research continues toward eliminating pathology, delaying any incapacitating decrement in function, and to determine biological mechanisms. The quantity of information, especially at the molecular and cellular levels is increasing. This research has provided some interesting clues.

Some enzyme activity goes down with age, some goes up.

The physical structure of the stuff of the older gene DNA is different than the young. Cells of older rats can't make RNA as fast as the younger, and some new kinds of RNA are found in older animals. Experiments with rats have prolonged vigorous life with reduced caloric intake. Antioxidants added to the diet of rats also appears to prolong life. The hypothesis upon which this procedure is based depends on the antioxidant inhibition of free radicals (such as OH or H_2O_2). Attack of free radicals upon membranes and enzymes, is said to be a process which damages the sac of digestive enzymes — the lysosomes, thus bringing about tissue destruction and probable lipofuscin formation.[20], [21] In cold blooded animals, a decrease in body temperature has even doubled the life span. Ability to synthesize hormones apparently changes little, but receptors on which they act may become less receptive effectively leaving the body with decreased efficiency in numerous hormone dependent processes. Cells of older animals in culture do not divide as many times as cells of younger animals.

Possibly the first two cases of genetic therapy and engineering have been reported: Two German girls suffering from a genetic disease lacked the enzyme arginase. Doctors injected a virus known to produce high levels of this enzyme. Final results have not yet been reported. In 1971, an experiment at the National Institute of Health tackled genetic errors. Scientists took skin cells from a patient with galactosemia, which is characterized by an inability to metabolize milk. A virus called lamda phage, which is able to synthesize the missing enzyme, was able to transfer the necessary genetic information so the cells could then synthesize the enzyme. An inborn error corrected!

We've come a long way from an "Alice in Wonderland" stance in the field of aging, and these techniques may conceivably be useful to modify some genetic program for aging (if indeed this is part of the aging causality) or remove some errors accumulated through a life cycle. The critical, qualitative step or steps are yet to be taken. However, even if they are far off, cohorts of older people in the near future are bound to be healthier, better educated, and have more expectations for a place in the society.

Perhaps much can be learned from the ancient Confucious, 500 B.C., who lived to be seventy-two. He might have been called the first theorist in age stratification. His theory of human development did not see the last part of life as inevitable senility, but as part of a continuum; indeed old age to him was life in its highest form:

"At 15, I applied myself to the study of wisdom. At 30, I grow stronger in it. At 40, I no longer have doubt. At 50, there was nothing on earth that could shake me, and at 70 I could follow the dictate of my heart without disobeying moral law."

REFERENCES

1. Guillerme, J. *Longevity.* New York: Walker and Co., 1963.
2. Gruman, J. "A History of Ideas about the Prolongation of Life; the Evolution of Elongation Hypotheses to 1800." In *Transactions of the American Philosophical Society. 56,* part 9, 1966.
3. Shock, N. "The Physiology of Aging." *Scientific American.* 206: 100-110, 1962.
4. Freeman, J.T. (ed.) *Clinical Features of the Older Patient.* Springfield, Ill.: Charles C. Thomas, 1965.
5. Chinn, A.B. "Physiology of Human Aging." In Birren, James (ed.) *Contemporary Gerontology: Issues and Concepts.* University of Southern California Press, 1972.
6. Makinodan, T., Perkins, E.H. and Chen, M.G. Immunologic Activity of the Aged. in Strehler, B. (ed.) *Advances in Gerontological Research. 3:* 171-198, 1965.
7. Hayflick, L. "Aging under Glass," *Experimental Gerontology. 5:* 291-303, 1970.
8. Hayflick, L. "The Limited *in vitro* Lifetime of Human Diploid Cell Strains," *Experimental Cell Research. 37:* 614-636, 1965.
9. Rahe, R., McKean, J.D. and Ransom, A.J. A Longitudinal Study of Life Changes and Illness Patterns. In *Journal of Psychosomatic Research. 10:* 355-366, 1967.
10. Palmore, E. and Jeffers, F.C. (eds.) *Prediction of Life Span, Recent Findings.* Lexington, Mass.: D.C. Health and Co., 1971.
11. a) Chebotarev, D. "Fight Against Old Age," *Gerontologist. 11,* (Part I), 359-361, 1971.
11. b) Sachuk, N., Population Longevity Study: Sources and Indices. *Journal of Gerontology. 25* (3), 262-264, 1970.
12. Butler, R. "The Destiny of Creativity in Later Life: Studies of Creative People and the Creative Process," in *Psychodynamic Studies on Aging.* Levin, S. and Rahana R., (eds.) New York: International University Press, 1967.
13. Davies, D. "A Shangri-La in Ecuador," *New Scientist.* pp. 236-238, February 1, 1973.
14. Leaf, A. "Every Day is a Gift When You are Over 100." *National Geographic. 143,* (1), 93-118, 1973.
15. Benet, S. "Why They Live to be 100, or even Older in Abkhasia," *New York Times Magazine.* pp. 3-34, December 26, 1971.
16. deVries, Herbert. "Physiological Effects of an Exercise Training Regimen Upon Men Aged 52-88," *Journal of Gerontology. 25,* 325-336, 1970.
17. Brody, H. "Structural Changes in the Aging Nervous System," in *Interdisciplinary Topics Gerontology.* Vol. 7, pp. 9-21. New York: Karger/Munchen, 1970.
18. Miller, R.G. "The Treatment of Osteoporosis," *Geront. Clin., 11,* 244-252, 1969.
19. Masters, W.H. and Johnson, V.E. *Human-Sexual Inadequacy.* Boston: Little, Brown, 1970.
20. Harman, D. "Free Radical Theory of Aging: Effect of the Amount and Degree of Unsaturation of Dietary Fat on Mortality Rate," *Journal of Gerontology. 26,* (4), 451-457, 1971.
21. Kohn, R.R. "Effect of Antioxidants on Life-Span of C57BL Mice," *Journal of Gerontology. 26,* (3), 378-380, 1971.

VI   THE SOCIOLOGY OF AGING:
Implications for the Helping Professions

*Vern L. Bengtson, Ph.D.**

There are four issues related to the sociology of aging that are of relevance for professionals who have responsibility for the aged. They are: loss, consequences, competence, and responsibility.

The first issue refers to *social loss* and involves the decline of interpersonal support, of a decent standard of living, and of a valued position in life. These aspects of an individual's social life change with the passage of time. The second theme, *consequences*, refers to the social-psychological results of these losses in the lives of normal older people. I want to suggest that not all of the consequences of social loss are negative. *Competence* refers to the adaptive capacity of the older person. Considered in the normal process of aging, competence can be judged in a variety of ways. I will argue that we pay attention to some of the less obvious of these. The fourth theme, *responsibility*, refers to some of the steps *we* as professionals must take in response to the first three issues. As members of the helping professions, or as citizens concerned with the problems faced by the elderly, we face a challenge to do more and to use greater imagination and insight than we have in the past.

I. SOCIOLOGY AND THE LIFE CYCLE

By way of introduction, let me discuss briefly the occult science of sociology and its relevance to the study of aging. Someone once said that sociology is the science that tells people what they know already in terms they cannot understand. I think it is true that we, as sociologists, have as our responsibility the explication of the obvious. As individuals grow up and assume adult responsibility, they come to have some common sense ideas and paradigms regarding their social world and its organization. Many of their observations are correct and some are patently wrong. Sociologists study social organization and interpersonal influence. They try to generate propositions about social behavior which are valid enough to stand the test of repeated analysis and investigation.

Sociologists study age in two ways. These two ways are quite different and yet they are complimentary (Bengtson, 1973). The first perspective in the sociology of age focuses on age as a

Associate Professor of Sociology, University of Southern California and Sociology Preceptor, Andrus Gerontology Center.

dimension of social organization and differentiation. This might be called the *macro* level of sociological analysis. It involves the study of large aggregates of humans, of nations and social institutions, such as the economy or the polity of communities and social networks. How is age a dimension of organization in these large aggregates?

At the national level, demographic analysis suggests some answers. Today we have over twenty million people who are above the age of 65. Many of these older people live at or below the poverty level; they have little power, little prestige, and little visibility. By the year 2005, when the World War II "baby boom" begins reaching retirement age, it has been projected that there will be almost forty million people above the age of 65 (Brotman, 1968). Just that increase in numbers alone will result in changes in social organization. What will be the effects of that increase on our beliefs, religious participation, and economic life? What will be the attributes of those individuals growing old in the year 2000? What sorts of bureaucracies, service agencies, and professional networks are going to be needed in order to accommodate such a large group of elderly individuals? Will the elderly represent a strong political force in our nation? These are the questions of social organization, the first perspective of sociology and aging (for an excellent overview, see Atchley, 1972).

The second way in which sociologists view age and aging is a social-psychological one. This *"micro"* sociology (Bengtson and Black, 1973) is probably more familiar to members of the helping professions than the macro-sociological view. This perspective analyzes changes in an individual's social world with the passage of time. As people grow up and grow old, their social world changes as does the way in which they view themselves.

Take, for example, the "career" of a woman as she progresses through various age-related positions in adulthood. In adolescence, she is unmarried and regarded as a non-adult. Then she falls in love and enters into a socially recognized contract, marriage. This represents the first major benchmark in what may be called her familial career. A second is when she gives birth to her firstborn child; a third when she sends that firstborn to school; a fourth when her first child leaves home as a young adult; and a fifth when all her children are grown or "launched." At this point, she may lose her husband; this is another important benchmark in the family career. By this time, she probably has become a grandparent; this is perhaps an important role for her or it may be a trivial one.

All careers, not only in the family but also in economic spheres, are marked by progressions through various positions. These positions have time boundaries associated with them. Sociologists are interested in studying the normal course of events in the lives of people as their social world contracts or expands with the passage of time.

Sociology, then, involves both studying age as a dimension of social organization and in terms of the changes that occur in an individual's social world with the passage of time. Recently, sociologists have tended to focus more and more on these issues of age (see Riley, 1971; Riley et al, 1972). And, more and more of the research done by professional sociologists is of relevance to members of the helping professions concerned with the aged (see Riley et al, 1971). What does this sociological research have to say about loss, consequences, competence, and responsibility, as these themes relate to aging?

II. LOSS

The first major issue I would like to discuss concerns loss. This is a theme which is touched upon in several of the papers in this volume. Physiologically, the period of old age involves the analysis of decrement and disease, as well as the special biological coping mechanisms the organism uses in adapting to these decrements. From a sociological perspective as well, the theme of loss and compensation is pervasive in the study of social changes over time. Irene Burnside (1970) has presented a perceptive analysis of loss as a dominant theme in the lives of older people who go to service agencies for help.

Looking at older people from a sociological perspective, there seem to be three kinds of loss. The first is *role* loss. Roles are, quite simply, the ways in which social positions are carried out by individual actors. As in a play, the script is there but the individual player reads the script in his own unique way. Each individual gives to the playing of that part a flavor which is different from what anyone else's interpretation would be. Sociologists investigate the ways in which the various roles mash or conflict in everyday life.

One can see the losses of social roles which occur with age most dramatically in retirement. There is also dramatic role loss in the lives of older women who become widows. Role loss occurs less visibly at the time of child launching. It involves the loss of an effective past function. This particular loss has not been studied extensively. But in the American society where there are many traditionally-oriented women, the major preoccupation of most women is the rearing and socializing of children. What happens when this role is taken away from them as their children become independent? This is a central theme for the many jokes about the interference of the mother-in-law. This issue even provides the subject matter for several current television series which attract a wide viewing audience. It is also the subject of some psychiatric investigation (Bart, 1968).

The second way in which loss can be viewed from a sociological perspective as one examines the lives of older people is in terms of *norms*. Norms are rules. They are the expectations which guide most of what we do in the course of an average day. Norms are obviously related to roles; there are the specific expectations concerning our activities in the work sphere, and with respect to parental and husband-wife roles. In short, we live our lives as a complex mixture of roles which have specific expectations. I've observed that the single role of wife involves the simultaneous performance of normative behaviors as cook, therapist, lover, mistress, chauffeur, manager, hostess, and housemaid.

What happens in the middle years when an individual begins to undergo the role changes we have been discussing? This means that expectations and norms also change. And, they change in a particular direction. They change toward a greater vagueness and lack of specificity. In other words, there is a loss of norms with time, just as there is loss of roles. For example in middle age, the individual is working and is the parent of dependent children. There are many expectations that govern our behavior in those roles. But when a person retires or loses a spouse the norms become much less specific. What *should* you do when you are retired? What *should* you do when your husband dies and you become widowed? There seem only to be expectations about what a person should not do. He should not expect to be socially active. He should probably try to forget about a sexual life. Women must not go out with any man much younger than they are. The movie "Harold and Maude" depicted in a tragic yet humorous way the relationship between an eighty-year-old woman and a seventeen-year-old boy. The reviews of that movie indicated that the movie was judged to be obscene by American audiences. Many viewers were repulsed and some were even nauseated by what they saw on the screen. American movie goers do not object to violence, or to blood and gore in a film; they do not object to flesh and nakedness, or to sexual explicitness. They do object, however, to an old woman and a young man in love, especially if that love is not platonic.

In our humor it is possible to see the norms which govern much of our everyday life. A current bumper sticker proclaims, "I'm not a dirty old man — I'm a sexy senior citizen." While the dirty old man may be humorous, the dirty old woman is not. Here is a norm of sexual loss that is inappropriate for many healthy older widows or widowers.

A third perspective from which sociologists might view loss

concerns changes in *reference group*. Much of our behavior is determined by the expectations of the groups to which we refer in judging our behavior. The work group or the professional group one identifies with is an important source of norms specifying appropriate behavior. The religious community a person identifies with is another significant source for our expectations. The friends a person has constitutes a third reference group.

So, what happens when the individual reaches the age of seventy and his friends begin to die? I once interviewed a man who had just celebrated his 104 birthday. He said to me, when we were talking about the problems of growing old, "You know, I haven't had a friend since I was 77. That's when my last friend died." Imagine living for 27 years without someone who is regarded as a friend! This represents loss of a confidant; of contact with an intimate; but also loss of reference group. What group can this man who is 104 years old refer to so he can judge the adequacy of his behavior? It is not appropriate for him to judge himself by the standards of middle life, but that is exactly what he does.

The lives of older people, therefore, can be characterized by a theme of loss. Sociologically, there is loss of social positions (roles), of expectations (norms), and of reference groups. What are some of the consequences of these losses in the lives of the older people?

III. CONSEQUENCES

Most of the investigators who write about the consequences of the loss of roles and norms in old age have emphasized the negative aspects of such loss. The first and perhaps greatest sociologist of the modern era was Emile Durkheim, who wrote penetrating studies of social organization and behavior in the late 19th century. He did a most brilliant analysis of suicide. What is it that causes people to take their own lives? What are the social causes of homocide? Durkheim, analyzing both demographic statistics and economic indicators, suggested that one cause of suicide is the feeling of loneliness coupled with the lack of clear-cut expectations resulting from a marginal social position. We know from more recent analysis that suicide is very often the result of a loss of roles, a loss of norms, and a loss of reference groups. It is perhaps no accident that in the older age groups, particularly among men, there is a sharp upsurge in the incidence of suicide.

How then might it be possible to compensate for the deleterious results of these social losses? This theme has intrigued many sociologists writing in the field of gerontology. Perhaps the most articulate proponent of one particular view is

Irving Rosow (1967, 1973). He suggests that the age homogenous housing environment — such as golden age apartments or "leisure world" developments — may be an effective way of ameliorating these losses in old age. Rosow's arguments are that older people in the context of American society are in a disadvantaged position with respect to roles and normative expectations. There are few socially-recognized roles for them and fewer norms guiding appropriate behavior in old age. By bringing aged individuals together, norms for appropriate or inappropriate behavior should increase in saliency. The result: the creation of an age-appropriate reference group. Anomie, or feelings of normlessness, will decrease. This suggests that places like Sun City or retirement hotels may be valuable contexts for socialization into old age and for the development of age-appropriate sets of expectations. Although the issue of age-segregated housing for the elderly is hotly debated, Rosow's data (1967) must be considered persuasive evidence of one alternative to the negative consequences of social loss in old age.

What are some *positive* consequences of the losses that occur with normal aging? This is a theme which has received little, if any, attention (see Schoenfeld, 1967). Usually, we look at old age only as a negative period of the life span. However, one consequence of decreases in the specific social expectations is an *increase in personal freedom.*

Consider the average fifty-five year old man and the way he spends his day. Eight to ten hours are devoted to working at a job which he may or may not be interested in, doing what others tell him to do. He may spend another few hours during the day worrying about his adolescent son who is dropping out and his daughter who is turning on. In addition, he is financially responsible for a houseful of consumers. This middle-aged man is governed by lots of roles and he has, as a consequence, relatively little freedom.

Look at the same man at age sixty-five. Now he is retired. There is no longer anyone to tell him how he should spend eight hours of his day. His kids are grown up. He no longer has the direct parental role, the responsibility for educating and launching the children. Although living on much less income, he has fewer financial responsibilities. In short, he has lost roles and has less clear-cut expectations. But, he has considerably more freedom and greater opportunity to do what he himself wants to do with his time. Loss represents potential gain.

Consider another loss, perhaps a more painful one: widowhood. I have known people who have suffered the loss of a spouse, who after a suitable period of mourning, have discovered a marvelous new life. Many marriages of long duration tend to be sufficiently unhappy so that they are not very pleasureful to those involved. The marriage relationship may have been so demanding that the personal creativity of each individual may have been hampered. The death of a spouse after a long and unsatisfying marriage may be the opportunity for many new kinds of freedom. Look at what is happening in our continuing education programs. A lot of the women who are enrolled are widows. When you query them closely, they seem to have felt uncomfortable about taking courses during their marriage. I am not suggesting that most middle-aged people long for widowhood, I am merely observing that in some cases the decrease in normative expectations can be viewed as an opportunity for gains in freedom and individual development. One of the myths of old age is that the social losses which are inevitable with the passage of time have only negative consequences. I am suggesting that there are positive results of such social losses in old age. Later on, I will make some specific suggestions about what professionals can do to highlight these positive consequences.

IV. COMPETENCE

The third major theme of this sociological perspective on aging is that of *competence*. This term has been under-utilized by those of us in the helping profession. Competence is perhaps a good synonym for that mysterious and euphemeral thing we have in mind when we talk about "mental health." I would also suggest that the term "competence" might be used as a good, one-word summary of what we as professionals hope to accomplish in our work related to the aged. *Enhancing the competence of older individuals* is our charge as professionals.

What is competence? It is a term we use frequently, yet it is perhaps hard to define. There are three definitions from the literature of social psychology that appear to relate to a discussion of aging (see Smith, 1969; Kuypers and Bengtson, 1973).

The first sociological definition treats competence as *adequate role performance.* We might say of a medical colleague, "He is really a competent surgeon." We mean that this individual performs the duties of that particular profession very well. We may say of another, "She is a very competent speaker." We mean, of course, that she performs that obligation quite well. Very often we stop there, not realizing that what is competence as defined by the social system (i.e. adequate role performance) may not be competence as defined by the individual. The surgeon may hate to get up in the middle of the night to perform an emergency surgery. He may have butterflies in his stomach and become tense and irritable every time he scrubs. The woman who appears to be such a competent speaker gets so nervous during her presentation that she is amazed the microphone does not pick up the sound of her knees knocking together. At times, those of us who perform competently as judged by the social expectations do not perform competently by our own definitions and standards of what we would like to be doing and why. This suggests a second definition of competence, one which stems from a more psychological orientation. Here competence is defined as *coping and doing what the individual himself wishes* to do. Competence is defined by the individual as a locus of his own humanistic values. A competent person is one who copes with the demands placed on him so that he receives maximum satisfaction from his activity (Kuypers Bengtson, 1973). This is different from competence determined strictly by the structure of the social system.

A third definition of competence is offered by M. Brewster Smith (1969). He defines competence as the *feeling of efficacy and coping*. It involves being able to manipulate the environment, being able to have an effect on the world. For an individual, to feel that he has an effect on the world is to feel competent.

I suggest here that competency is the key to understanding successful aging. Our goal as helping professionals should be to increase the competency of elderly individuals. I think professionals do a fairly good job in terms of the first definition of competence; we do try to encourage adequate role performance among the elderly. Therapy, whether physical, psychological, or occupational, has to do with helping people cope effectively with situations in their external environment. Professionals deal less well with the second definition, that of helping older people to do what they themselves choose to do. Also, it seems that we have not turned our full attention to the third definition, to helping people have feelings of efficacy and competence when they are aged. Perhaps it is here that we should begin examining our responsibilities as members of the helping professions.

V. RESPONSIBILITY

We have conceptualized some sociological perspectives of aging as loss of social roles, norms, and reference groups. We have explored the negative and positive consequences of these losses. Some alternative definitions of competence have been proposed as goals toward which our helping actions might be directed. What is our responsibility as professionals interested in the aging process? I would like to suggest that we have four responsibilities. Often at conferences and meetings, members of the helping professions get together to talk about things they should be doing. I hope that we can stop talking and begin doing in ways that make a difference in our effectiveness as professionals.

I would like to suggest that our first responsibility is to *acknowledge continuity as well as decrement* in the lives of older people. There is continuous coping as well as steady loss in older people. Recognizing this, we would probably have a more realistic picture of the processes of aging. No one becomes suddenly old. Aging is a gradual process. In our professional roles we often sit across a desk interviewing an older person who is in trouble. We know about the losses he has experienced. It is more difficult for us to view the resources present in the life of this older person. We must remember that he or she has spent a lifetime coping with problems. The individual's way of coping might be used to alleviate crises. So, let's acknowledge continuity as well as decrement, strength as well as decline.

Second, it is our responsibility to *recognize the creativity and the freedom* involved in the process of growing old. We must recognize that the loss of roles and clear-cut expectations results in greater freedom and time for exploration. I think we are closer to understanding the aging process if we recognize this. It might be helpful for us to point out the opportunity for increased freedom to the aging individual. Often it is difficult to see the advantages of retirement, and especially of widowhood. In part, it is culturally prohibited for us to think about old age in positive terms. If a person is not working, so many people have told me, he is a bum and others will regard him as such. We need to point to the freedom and the creativity which even losses might bring to the lives of older people.

The third responsibility we have is to *promote change* in much broader terms than we have in the past. In another paper a colleague and I have described a "social reconstruction system" of aging (Kuypers and Bengtson, 1973; Bengtson, 1973). There are many things that we as a nation are now ready to recognize with respect to improving the conditions of the elderly. For example, there is a growing awareness of the truly astonishing population revolution in our society. The number of people over the age of 65 has increased from four million in 1900 to twenty million in 1970. This demographic revolution must necessarily have associated with it a service revolution, especially in this society where the average family does not care for its aged.

It is our responsibility to advocate, to agitate, and politicize for the programs needed by elderly people. It is sad that programs in aging are among the first to suffer budget cuts, especially at the county level. We need to recognize that the aged have potential political strength. Certainly, fourteen to fifteen million voters above the age of sixty-five offer a promise of political power. The national organizations, such as the

American Association of Retired Persons (AARP) or the National Council of Senior Citizens (NCSC), could become strong political forces. We need to band together to advocate for the needs of aged individuals. These are humanitarian concerns which transcend party lines.

Finally, I would like to suggest that we need to *give more responsibility to the aged themselves.* This way, our efforts to enhance their own competence will be more effective. Remember that competence can be defined as a *feeling* of efficacy; and it can also be defined as doing what you want to do. How often do we as professionals allow people to decide for themselves what they want to be doing? It is true that we may lose some of our own power, as well as some time and efficiency. We may also sense that we are not helping if we let the elderly do what they want to. But really, there is no loss, there are only gains as older people become more competent. Imagine a home for older people run entirely by a board of residents. In this home, the middle-aged professionals have only the caretaker responsibilities specified by the residents themselves. Imagine a program in continuing education where older people determine the courses offered. In the year 2000 many more healthy and virile older people will be in the senior citizen category. They should not be forced into an unnecessary dependent position. Older people ought to be free to choose their own interests. This freedom has two consequences: (1) elderly people will define what is right for them; (2) having the freedom to choose, they will feel more competent. If competence is our goal as professionals, we can come closer to this goal by divesting ourselves of our traditional responsibilities and by giving these to the aged.

CONCLUSION

I have discussed loss and its consequences, some alternative definitions of competence, and suggested new responsibilities for the helping professionals. These are all themes relevant to a sociological perspective of aging. My hope is that we will take this opportunity to redefine our responsibility toward increasing the competence of the elderly. We must begin to perceive old age as the increased opportunity for growth and development, not just a time of decline and loss.

REFERENCES

Atchley, R.N. *The Social Forces in Later Life: An Introduction to Social Gerontology.* Belmont, California: Wadsworth Publishing Co., 1972.

Bart, P. Social Structure and Vocabularies of Discomfort: What Happened to Female Hysteria? *Journal of Helath and Social Behavior,* 1968, 9, 188-193.

Bengtson, V.L. *The Social Psychology of Aging.* Indianapolis, Indiana: Bobbs-Merrill, 1973.

Bengtson, V.L. and K.D. Black. Inter-generational Relations and Continuities in Socialization. In P. Baltes and W. Schaie (Eds.), *Life-span Developmental Psychology: Personality and Socialization.* New York: Academic Press, 1973.

Birren, J.E. *The Psychology of Aging.* New York: Prentice Hall, 1964.

Brotman, H.B. Who are the Aged: A Demographic View. *Occasional Papers in Gerontology,* University fo Michigan, 1968, *1.*

Burnside, I.M. Loss: A Constant Theme in Group Work with the Aged. *Hospital and Community Psychiatry,* 1970, *21* (6), 173-177.

Kuypers, J.A. and V.L. Bengtson. Competence and Social Breakdown: A Social-Psychological View of Aging. *Human Development,* 1973, 16 (2), 177-189.

Neugarten, B.L. *Middle Age and Aging: A Reader in Social Psychology.* Chicago: University of Chicago Press, 1968.

Riley, M.W. Social Gerontology and the Age Stratification of *Society. Gerontologist,* 1971, 11 (1), 79-87.

Riley, M.W., M. Johnson, and A. Foner. *Aging and Society, Vol. III: A Sociology of Age Stratification.* New York: Russell Sage Foundation, 1972.

Rosow, I. *Social Integration of the Aged.* New York: The Free Press, 1973.

Rosow, I. *Socialization into old age.* Berkeley: University of California Press, 1973.

Smith, M.B. *Social Psychology and Human Values.* Chicago: Aldine, 1969.

Schoenfeld, D.A. Geronting: Reflections on Successful Aging. *Gerontologist,* 1967, 7 (4), 270-273.

VII   THE OLDER PERSON AND THE FAMILY

*Dean Black, Ph.D.**

Discussing the family is a challenge for anyone because the topic is so very broad. There is so much to say that one hardly knows where to begin. A second problem in talking to others about families is that almost everyone lives in families. It may surprise you when I say that our living in families could be a problem. When I give talks, however, it often is. It's so easy for people to say either, "I already knew that. Why can't you tell me something new?" Or else, "You don't know what you are talking about. I have lived in a family all my life, and it never happened that way."

The family is important. I am sure that all of you know that. I know it, not only from my academic study of family sociology, but from many aspects of my own experience. For example, whenever I tell someone that I am a gerontologist, I get either one of two reactions. Some people react as did a man I met recently in a Sunday School class. He asked then, as do so many, "What in the world is Gerontology?" When I told him, he got one of those looks on his face that said something like, "I wish you never told me." I understand why he said that when I asked him what he did for a living. He was a mortician. The other common reaction to my work is one that lets me know people are concerned about their families and about their old people. So often, when I tell people that I study aging, they step closer and, almost in a confidential tone, say to me, "I am so happy that I have had a chance to meet you. Can you tell me what I should do about mother?"

There is an interesting thing that lets us know family ties are important to older people. That is the very common existence of what we call "fictive kin." Fictive kin are people you pretend are related to you, even though they are not. Perhaps we can all remember as children that we had various "aunts" and "uncles" who were adult friends of our parents. Such fictive kin are actually quite common. In a class I once had, I asked my students how many of them had an older person whom they called by a family title, even though there was no actual blood relationship. Over one half of the students raised their hands. When I questioned them further, I discovered that for many of those young people, those relationships were as meaningful as the relationships they shared with actual blood kin. This

*Assistant Professor of Sociology, University of Southern California.

willingness of people to create family relationships where none previously existed has been used by the government to develop an effective program for helping both older people and young children. This is the Foster Grandparents Program. This program helps elderly men and women overcome many of the problems that seem to accompanying aging: loneliness, a feeling of uselessness, and so on. The older person becomes involved as a foster grandparent with a child who needs the warmth and benefits of a close personal relationship. Since the program was started in about 1966, it has experienced dynamic growth. It has demonstrated very convincingly the importance to both young and old of a family type relationship, whether it be artificially established or the product of a blood relationship.

I would like to emphasize that the family is not a single, readily recognizable, entity. The family is many things. A well known family sociologist, Marvin Sussman, wrote an article in 1971 in which he identified something like twenty different family forms. New family forms are continually evolving in this time of rapid social change. For a practitioner working with older people, the "family" is usually not difficult to define. The family consists of the people who brought the older person to the facility; it includes those who come to visit. The family members are also often defined as those who are financially responsible for the older person's care. Of course, what I have described here is really a very limited segment of the older person's entire family. Service providers probably deal most often, for example, with a daughter rather than a son. Women seem to maintain parent-child ties more than men do. And the issues dealt with are apt to be somewhat limited as well. For example, the children must be helped to handle their guilt. They feel guilty and insecure because they have to bring the older person into the facility. They need help to work that through. There are other things. Some family members don't know how to visit properly. It may be that Mom used to be the sounding board for all of the family problems. So, when the children come to visit they bare their souls and their griefs to Mom. After they feel better, they leave. Mom may feel better too, if she has gained a sense of usefulness from the experience. But it can also be a depressing, damaging experience for her. So families sometimes must be taught to be good visitors. Another problem often arises if the older person is released from a convalescent facility. We often speak of the problems the older person has in adapting to his release. Since the older person is most often released into the family, that family has to be prepared to take the older person back.

Each of us has had a limited experience with families, and so we also have a somewhat limited perspective. Yet I think we can better serve older people and their families by recognizing that there are a great variety of family forms, and that the particular nature of your challenge with the older person and the family is a product of the nature of the entire family of the older person you serve.

Many older people live alone. Of those who live alone, a small percentage have no family still living. Most of those with no living family are probably found among the eight percent of those sixty-five and over who have never married. The others have simply outlived the other members of their family. It is apparent that this group of older people includes many widows. There are over eleven million widowed persons in the United States today, and three-fourths of those are over the age of sixty-five. Every year, 251,000 men and 592,000 women are widowed. Widowhood is a severe crisis. In fact, a group of researchers who were studying the impact of many events involving a change in a person's life discovered that death of a spouse was rated as the most severe crisis event that could be encountered in life. Nevertheless, most widowed persons are not left totally alone and do have other living relatives, although they may not share the same household with them. Of those sixty-five and over, seventy-five to eighty percent have living children. Statistics show that even more of them have living siblings. One study reported that eighty-two percent of their respondents had living siblings. A slightly greater percentage of them reported living children. This can be partially explained by the greater family size of a few generations ago, but it is an amazing thing nevertheless.

More common than the single aged individual is the aging couple. Sixty-eight percent of men and thirty-four percent of women over sixty-five are married. Two thirds of those who are married live independently of other family members; that is, although they may have other living relatives — siblings and children, for example — they do not share their household with them. The figures I just cited reflect the much higher number of widowed women than men. There are, of course, two reasons for this. First, women tend to outlast men, and so the chances of a woman losing her husband are greater than are his chances of losing her. The second factor is the phenomenon of remarriage. In the fairly recent past, remarriage was less an acceptable option for the older person who is widowed than it is today. People tended to feel that the sexual aspects of marriage were no longer of interest to the elderly, an idea that has since been discredited by researchers from Kinsey to Masters and Johnson. Often, an older person who wanted to marry again would find that society looked at that idea with disapproval. His friends, his children, and the larger community might discourage his remarriage as being somehow foolish and improper. Although the general public has still not fully accepted the idea that marriage in the later years is appropriate, social barriers against remarriage are breaking down, particularly for men. If the trend continues, there may yet be a time when remarriage is not only an accepted but an expected event for both men and women following the death of a spouse.

There are still other older persons who live in what might be called a multi-generation or complex family household. Thirty-six percent of elderly people live with their children; ten percent live with their siblings; and, amazingly, as many as five percent of elderly people over sixty-five live with aging parents.

Many children undoubtedly expect to have their parents live with them when they become unable to take care of themselves. They probably feel as well that this would be expected and desired by their parents. However, research has shown that only about eight percent of elderly people feel that it is desirable to live with their children. In one study, seventy-seven percent of the elderly people interviewed, said they would choose to live somewhere other than with their children when they are no longer able to care for themselves. I once mentioned this fact to a friend of mine, and she said, "but they only say that because they feel they will be a burden. I have that problem with my mother. She insists that she doesn't want to come to live with us, but I know that it is only because she feels it would be hard on us."

What my friend means by this was that the figures I cited were misleading. She feels that older people may say that they don't want to live with their children, but underneath they really do. I think I would tend to disagree with her. Parents often genuinely do not want to live with children though the children do not believe that their reasons are acceptable. An older person who feels he is being a burden will be miserable whether he is actually being a burden or not. And children who persist in saying things like, "But mother, I told you time and again that I don't mind taking care of you," can often do little to relieve the older person's anxieties. Under conditions like that, it is not unreasonable that they should want to live with someone they feel would not be overburdened by their presence.

I have been concerned so far with different family forms. There are single older people living alone, some with no living family, some never married, some widowed, some with living children, some with living siblings, and so on. There are aging couples, some with their spouse of half a century, some newlyweds, and even some who may merely be continuing a lifelong pattern of one marriage after another. Then there are multi-generational families, helpful in so many ways, and yet a potential source of anxiety to young and old alike.

There are still other important differences between families. Those are the result of ethnic and cultural differences. For example, I recently heard a very interesting talk by a psychologist who grew to her adult years on the Chinese mainland; her name is Dr. Yung-Hua Liu, and she is now with the Student Counseling Center at U.C.L.A. She pointed out to us that the attitude of the young towards the old in China is very different than it is here in our country. She stated that one important reason for this is the philosophical heritage that all Chinese children of her era learned by word of mouth from their parents. That philosophy speaks very directly of the value of old age. For example, she cited one of the sayings of Confucius which went something like this:

At 15, I applied myself to the study of wisdom,
At 30, I grew stronger in it,
At 40, I no longer had doubt,
At 50, there was nothing on earth that could shake me,
At 70, I could follow the dictate of my heart without disobeying moral law.

Can you see what this teaches them about their old people? Another important influence on the Chinese attitude towards aging is their vocabulary. In English, our word, "old," often has a negative connotation. But in Chinese, the word for "old" has a neutral value, and even tends toward a positive kind of feeling. I believe Dr. Liu said the word was "lao." She told us that the word is rarely used by itself, but is rather used in combination with other words to form new words with very different meanings. For example, when combined with another word, it means honesty. And she went on to list other words that could be formed with the Chinese word for old. All of them were words that almost invariably referred to things of honor and value. Beyond these philosophical and linguistic factors which make old age a positive thing can be added the practice of ancestor worship. Ancestor worship brings reverence for old age and things old directly into the family context. Ancestor worship anchors family roots deep in historial time, living and dead, within the Chinese family. I believe that this example serves to illustrate the fact that the cultural heritage can greatly influence the nature of an older person's experience within a family, and the feelings of family members toward the older person.

There are indeed many family forms, and the family can mean many different things to different people. But in spite of the variations, there are some general features of families that

73

are important to the understanding of the role of the family in later life. The first feature has to do with the sort of personal relationships that exist in families. The second feature has to do with the way the family can organize itself as a help-giving unit. Family relationships are personal; they are face-to-face; they are intimate relationships. They are relationships in which the people are important, and not the positions they hold. In order to understand this more clearly, let me contrast the personal, intimate family relationship with the sort of relationship which exists in a bureaucratic institution. For example, when you go into a bank, you expect a teller to help you. Suppose that in the middle of the transaction, someone taps your teller on the shoulder and tells him that he had a telephone call, then steps into the teller's window and says to you, "Hello, I am Mr. Wilson. The other teller had to answer a telephone call." This probably would not bother you. If it did, your main concern would be this: does Mr. Wilson know how to be a teller? If he does, there is no reason to worry; the important thing is that he know how to carry out the position of being a teller. In contrast, suppose a child goes home one afternoon after school, walks into the house, and meets a strange lady who says, "Hello there. Your mother has been transferred to another family, and I am here to take her place. Don't worry; I know all about being a mother. I can cook, wash clothes, and do everything a mother must do." Will the child accept that? Would you accept it? Of course not! Because in a family the people are important, not what they do. And this is why families are undoubtedly the source of our most meaningful, personal relationships. And the same intimacy is the reason why in the family comes some of the most destructive inter-personal violence. We have all seen examples of the strength of the family bond. I recall seeing a well known poster that showed a small child carrying another little boy. The caption read something like, "He ain't heavy, Mister, he is my Brother." Once on the television show, "Leave it to Beaver," Beaver saw a boy and a girl fighting. In the best tradition of chivalry, little Beaver stepped in to break it up. Suddenly he found himself being attacked by both children. You see, they were brother and sister, and, even though they fought, the bond between them was strong enough to make them unite against anything that threatened either one of them.

These were examples using children, but what they illustrate persists throughout life. The evidence shows that the family is still a very important source of meaningful social interaction for the elderly. Research studies have found things like this: sixty-two percent of people aged sixty-five and over have a son or a daughter within walking distance; eighty-four percent live within one hour of at least one of their children; and only seven percent live further away than two hours. Family members are generally quite available to an older person as a source of interaction.

But you might ask whether or not they take advantage of their availability. One study found that sixty-five percent of the older people studied had seen at least one of their children during the previous twenty-four hours; and over eighty percent had seen at least one child in the preceding week. It is apparent that the family is indeed a key source of social interaction during the later years. That is not to say that interaction is always positive; in fact, one study showed that older women who live near a married child who had young children, tended to have low morale. I guess grandmother can be asked to be a babysitter once too often. Another study showed that one of the main reasons why people in the lower classes moved from one city to another was to get away from the close contact of their kin. Whether the interaction is positive or negative, or as is more likely the case, whether it has both positive and negative aspects, the family is an important and meaningful source of social support during the later years.

The second general feature has to do with the family as a help-giving unit. Again, a contrast with a bureaucracy will help to illustrate this. Bureaucratic organizations have a fixed, inflexible schedule of activities for handling certain pre-defined problems. Since they have handled about every problem that could come up, they have also devised set ways of doing things. If someone comes along with an unusual problem, the response is likely to be, "I am sorry; we don't handle that sort of thing." But, families are not like that. They are flexible; they are diffuse in their activities and have no specific single purposes. As a result, the family is very often able to handle emergencies that demand speed of action and flexibility in a much better way than can the service bureaucracies.

After the major flood that hit Denver in the early sixties, some people did a study to find out what were the victims' major sources of help. They wondered: do people rely on the service agencies provided for them by the local, state and national governments? Or, do they rather seek the help of friends, neighbors, and kin? They found that family and kin were by far the most important source of aid. People tended to go to the more formalized service agencies only as a last resort. The reason, again, is that the family is a flexible kind of organization that can quickly mobilize itself around a particular problem. This flexibility is, of course, supported by the kind of intimate feeling for one another I spoke of earlier. This sort of thing has been found in study after study. I don't feel it is necessary to burden you here with the details of research. It is enough, I believe, to simply point out that there is overwhelming evidence for a two-way pattern of help and support flowing between the older and the younger generations in American families. The aid may be in the form of money or services, it may be a response to an immediate and potentially destructive crisis, or it may be an integral part of the pattern of daily life. But, whatever the form, there is little doubt that the family is the most important source of aid for the majority of older people today. There is one more thing regarding the family as a source of help that often tends to be ignored. That is the fact that some old people have a great capacity to tyranize their families. I read of one instance of an eighty-two year old father of five, named Mr. Jones. He had been a successful businessman, and, as a result, was well-off financially and accustomed to having his orders obeyed. His wife died a few years before, and since he was in a wheel chair, he needed someone to take care of him. He demanded that his forty-five year old bachelor son give up his job and move in to become his caretaker. This seemed to be a reasonable solution to everyone, because Buddy did not like his job anyway. So, Buddy became his dad's nurse, with an allowance of $50.00 a week, a new car, and free board and room. But the problem is that now, after several years, the arrangement still goes on. Dad is completely satisfied and refuses to even consider any other arrangement. But what will happen to Buddy when his father finally dies? Will he have a chance to get a job again? Mr. Jones may have felt that the arrangement was ideal, but the cost to Buddy could be very great indeed.

Patriarchal tyrrany was the theme of the movie, "I Never Sang for my Father." In that movie, the middle-aged son of an elderly father wanted to get married again following a period of widowerhood. But the father clung to his son. It was as though his life depended upon whether or not he could prevent his son from marrying once again and moving into a home of his own. The movie traced the course of this struggle, which eventually erupted into a final, bitter and angry separation.

I have now traced two important meanings of the family to an older person. The family is a source of intimate social relationships. It is also the most important source of help in time of need. But there is another, perhaps more subtle, meaning of the family that is well illustrated in a screen play that was written by Dick Eribes that is called, "I Remember the Future as Though It Were Yesterday." It tells of an elderly father who was moving from the large home where he had raised his family and seen his wife pass away, into some kind of retirement housing, where he couldn't take along many of the things that seemed to collect in houses where children grow up.

So he had a garage sale, and one of his sons, who was by now a middle-aged man, was helping him to get things set up for the sale. They placed everything out on tables in the front yard, and soon the people began to come. The father and the son played two different roles in the drama that began to unfold. The son was the bargainer. He would talk to the people and try to get the prices up. He took very seriously the idea that he could best serve his father by helping him raise money that was so important now during his retirement years. The father didn't look at all like a salesman. In fact, he walked around like a customer, picking up the various articles, looking them over as though he were considering which one to buy. A little boy came along and began to look at a bicycle that had once belonged to the old man's son. The old man watched him for awhile and then bent down beside the boy and said, "You know, my boy used that bike when he was your age." The little boy said, "Gosh, it sure is a nice bike." The father said, "How would you like to have that bike?" The little boy said, "Oh, I wish I could, but I haven't got enough money." And, then the father stood up and said to the boy, "You don't have to pay for it; I want you to have it. Go on, take it. Get on it and let me see how you can ride it." And off the boy rode.

The son was angry. "Dad," he said, "I could have gotten $20.00 for that bike." You see, he didn't understand what the father was doing. The old man had created for himself a bit of a future out of the past. He had taken something out of his past and given it a future in that little boy. "I Remember the Future as Though It Were Yesterday."

People seek immortality in a variety of ways. Some believe in an after-life; some hope for monuments and physical evidences of their life. But for many, their future exists only as a part of them carried on by those who bear their name.

I'd like to close by drawing your attention to something that Irving Goffman talks about in his book called, *Asylums.* When Goffman talks about "Asylums," he is referring to the whole variety of institutions where people go to be protected from intrusions of the world outside, and so that the world outside might be protected from them. In many ways, institutions for the aged can be considered as such total institutions. Goffman speaks of the "stripping" process that people are often required to undergo as they enter an institution. They are stripped of many things. Sometimes, it is the clothing they wear; often it will be what Goffman calls "The Identity Kit," a comb, a mirror, make-up; or, it may be things like clocks or books. But, whatever it is, it is virtually certain that an older person must lose some things as he comes into an institution. There simply is not enough space for everything he once had. But, there are some things that cannot be taken away from an older person, and I believe that the most important of these is this: Every older person that you encounter is a person with a history in a family. For most older people, that family is still the most important aspect of their social world.

VIII   ENVIRONMENTAL INFLUENCES ON THE OLDER PERSON

*Robert Newcomer**

When we are concerned about environmental influences, we must consider two basic questions: What do we mean by environment? What do we need to understand about the older person when we evaluate possible environmental affects on him? This paper will attempt to present a broad framework in which to view environmental influences on behavior and some specific findings which can be translated into your daily work.

DEFINING ENVIRONMENT

There are countless definitions of environment; one of the most comprehensive has been postulated by Powell Lawton (1970). According to Lawton, five components define the environment: (1) The *individual* component includes personality, perceptual and cognitive skills, lifetime experiences, and physical capability, (2) The *interpersonal environment* includes family and friends and others from whom the individual takes cues, (3) The *supra-personal environment*, a less clear component, refers to the predominating social characteristics of a setting. For example, if we have a nursing home and we bring in people from a mental hospital, what effect does this have on the people who are currently living in that nursing home? Up to a point, it may have no effect. But as you increase the number of such people, something about the atmosphere may change. By just looking around them, the original patients will see more people with low mental competence and they may suddenly start expecting themselves to be less capable. This is just one illustration of how a super-personal environment may influence what we do and feel. (4) The fourth component is *social norms and rules*. The administrative policy of a home, a convalescent hospital, or whatever, imposes certain kinds of standards about how they expect people to behave. But, also our society and our culture impose upon us rules about what is appropriate and what is not appropriate behavior. This is seen in a hospital where the patients themselves develop norms about what is acceptable or what is not acceptable behavior. (5) The final component is the *physical environment* itself, such as the furniture or the room, the temperature, and any number of other physical attributes.

With five components, an evaluation of environments and

*Preceptor, Urban and Regional Planning, Andrus Gerontology Center, University of Southern California.

environmental influences becomes a complicated task. This complexity is compounded by the fact that environments exist on a hierarchy of scales. Let me illustrate this for you. If separate groups of people are seated at tables in a room, each of those tables produces a behavioral setting. And yet, the whole room is also a behavioral setting, but on a different scale. What if a group at one table suddenly started to sing instead of talk as the others in the room were doing? We would have seen how one environmental scale could have influenced each of the other small groups and ultimately how it could have influenced all of the behavior in the room. This is just part of the complexity of environmental influences of which we must be aware.

INFLUENCES ON BEHAVIOR

Environment can influence behavior when an individual's capabilities are matched against his environmental situation. Like each of you, the environment may have relatively little effect on a very capable person who may be able to change the environment and change his situation. If the situation is something he is not pleased with, something overtaxing him, something that is not stimulating enough, he leaves. However, as an individual's capabilities decrease, he may have less of a possibility to manipulate the situation. When one considers the institutionalized, it is obvious that the individual's alternatives are even more constrained. Assistance must be provided for a patient who is too weak to lean from his bed to the bedside table for a drink of water. Taking a drink is the behavior in question. Other patients can provide it, or the staff can provide it, or the water can be moved to the overbed tray so that the person can get it himself. Each of these small differences in how an individual is supported by his environment illustrates a match-up between capability and situation.

How an environment can provide support is a very important question from the standpoint of staff. Often overlooked is the importance of the way in which services are provided and their effects on the patients. By not allowing him to perform tasks that he is capable of performing; it is possible to erode capability by requiring individuals to do things they are not really capable of doing. There are no clear-cut techniques for knowing precisely which level of support is the best for a particular individual in a particular situation. There are, however, some simple questions we should ask each time we find ourselves in a situation of matching people and environments. Essentially these questions concern the relationship between the environment and the four basic psychosocial needs of man: order, identity, social connectedness, and effectance.

DEFINING PSYCHO-SOCIAL NEEDS

(1) The need for *order* is simply the recognition that for a person to function and to orient in an environment, he must be able to put it into some context of experience. Order permits people to know what an environmental situation is asking of them and to find the appropriate response to it. The cautiousness in the behavior of older persons is in part a consequence of decreasing sensory capability and of the reliance on non-habilnal ways of processing information about the situation. (2) The need for *identity* is very closely related to the need for order. Now the person is saying to himself, "How do I fit into this situation? How am I different? What makes me special?" (3) *Social connectedness* refers to the need for control over the intensity and quality of social contact with other individuals. (4) *Effectance* refers to the individual's need to have impact on his environment, to manipulate the environment and to have some sense of control.

How can we operationally apply these needs in our daily work? Let's start with order. How does what we are doing or providing affect the patient's ability to order his surroundings? To illustrate: if a person has never been to a social agency before, but now needs to see a social worker, we can recommend a social worker for him to visit. But, maybe it would be wiser to spend the time to take the patient ourselves. This would help the individual find out how the system works, and orient him to the situation. He could more easily gain some cognitive order during a very strange and threatening first encounter. There are other examples to show how identity is affected if the individual's capability does not match up to the demands of the task. We might ask how social connectedness relationships and effectance interrelate with the structure of the physical environment. Remembering my geriatric ward experiences for a moment, let me relate to you a case of extreme insensitivity to these basic psycho-social needs. We had a patient in his late fifties who, because of some undiagnosed disease, was completely paralyzed. All he could move were his eyes. He could not talk because of a tracheotemy. How was this patient cared for? He was routinely turned every 2 hours and upon demand. He was bathed daily, his bedding was changed as needed, and he was fed through a gastric tube. How do you react to that? In a professional sense, this man was given adequate care. He had no bed sores, and he was alive. Yet, if we consider his treatment against the psycho-social needs perspective, the injustice to this man is unhuman. Noone spoke to him, except when providing service. Volunteers didn't come to visit or read. No radio or television was provided to break up the monotony of this man's day. He was not taken outside either in a wheelchair, or in a bed. He had few visitors. This man was not a mental vegetable, but treatment was accorded as if he were.

How often in our routine professional functioning do we neglect the broader needs of our patients? How simple it would be to evaluate our service for each patient or client in the terms I've discussed here! We must ask, does our treatment affect a patient's sense of order, identity, social connectedness and effectance? How could I alter my method of service delivery to better service these needs? There is much talk today of expanding the therapeutic functions of nurses. Here is a good place to begin.

There is one more aspect of the complexity that is part of any attempt to match people to environments. It is important to realize that the psycho-social needs are interrelated. This means that maximizing the fulfillment in one need may have negative consequences on another. As an example, consider the situation of an old woman living out in the community who is no longer able to cook adequately for herself and whose house is really too large for her to maintain and keep clean. Using the social service alternatives available, we can bring in hot meals and a housekeeper. This woman's sense of order is probably going to remain very high, because she is in familiar surroundings. Nothing is changed, except she has someone coming to help. Her sense of identity may stay very high if she believes that remaining in the community is a symbol of independence. One need affected in a negative way might be her sense of social connectedness. This woman might not be able to attain the social interaction she desires from other people who would be available for only a few hours a day or a few hours a week. Her sense of effectance could be affected even more adversely. A second alternative that we might consider for this woman would be to remove her from this house and place her in congregate housing. The woman would live in a small apartment and go to a central dining room for her meals. This apartment would be small enough for the woman to maintain herself. And, because this woman is able to take care of herself in a slightly better manner than previously, her sense of effectance should go up. Also, I think her level of social connectedness would increase, because of the availability of more social interaction in this new setting. Whether the loss of identify associated with leaving her house and being institutionalized is outweighed by the other gains is a problematic issue that must be evaluated on an individual basis. The point is that psycho-social needs are affected differently by alternative means of service delivery. We should be thinking about all the consequences and tradeoffs that have to be made.

TERRITORIALITY, PERSONAL SPACE AND PRIVACY.

Having introduced a few basic concepts, let's shift the focus now to the substantive areas of privacy and territoriality. To a large extent, these two constructs of privacy and territoriality cut across the psyco-social needs of order, identity, social connectedness and effectance.

What is meant by territoriality? Territoriality, as investigated by anthropologists (Hall, 1966 and Sommers, 1969) and others is essentially a spatial notion. In other words, man has a sense of what distance between himself and another individual means. Being very close, touching, and even feeling another's breath signifies a very intimate contact within our territorial space. A second level of this personal distance is termed personal space. This is the space that is within an arm's length of one's own body. This distance might be used for whispering or similar private conversation. A more normal conversational distance is about an arm's length away. This we call the social-casual distance. To illustrate our sensitivity to these spatial dimensions, let's consider something we've all experienced when talking to people. Sometimes we feel that we are too far away and move a little closer to them. If the other person is too close, we might find ourselves moving backward to adjust to a more comfortable distance. In extreme situations where two people have different senses of appropriate distance, they might quite literally chase each other around the room. The final, distinct spatial distance category is public aggressive distance. Public aggressive distance is distance beyond the range for comfortable conversation. My relationship to an audience is a public aggressive distance. When you walk into a room, and first spot someone across the room and gesture to him, that too involves a public aggressive distance. In normal situations, we proceed through a sequencing of these distances. We go from the public aggressive to the social casual, to the personal, and to the intimate. Violations of this sequencing can be very stressful. It has been found in mental patients, for example, that violations cause real agitation and anger. Looking back at my own experience as a nurses' aid, I remember the countless times that I violated my patient's sense of personal space. I'd walk up to the side of their bed, perhaps to turn them over, without even calling their name to alert them that I was coming. Who knows what effect or stress this generates in the individual as such lack of consideration continues day in and day out? Such stress could be avoided if staff are sensitive to the "needs" of their patients.

Let's consider now how territoriality affects the way people behave in space. Imagine a room with furniture in it. Have you ever paid much attention to the way people sit around tables, or couches, or their bed, or even around a room? Considering just tables, there are square ones, rectangular ones, round ones. Each of these tables functions differently to invite or discourage social interaction. Round tables invite social interaction. You can sit in any one spot, and a person can sit anywhere else at that table. The other person does not have to be looking straight at you, but he has the option of turning towards you to make eye contact and start a conversation. Being in control of eye contact gives each person involved a sense of privacy. With a rectangular table, some of these options are excluded. Most conversations at a rectangular table occur when people are sitting adjacent to each other at a corner, not when they are sitting directly across from each other. The main reason again is because this sense of visual privacy afforded by the adjacent position. Also, the adjacent corner position is the more comfortable conversational distance.

Often, seating arrangements of a lounge or common space in our institutional housing projects are not designed to respect patient's needs for privacy or to facilitate social interaction. In a typical lobby of an institution, you see a straight line of benches. This happens because such arrangements look nice, not because they are usable. What do I mean by usable? When there is a straight line bench, or when three chairs are lined up in a row, it is very hard for people at the ends to talk to each other if someone is between them. The people on the ends can't make good eye contact. It is important to sit next to another person in order to maintain the appropriate eye contact for a conversation.

The manner in which we arrange ourselves on furniture (Sommers, 1969) communicates information to other people. Where we sit is a signal to others as to whether they are invited to join us or not. When you sit towards one of the arms on a couch, you are inviting someone to come and join you. At least you are not telling everyone to stay away. If you want to take that couch for yourself, you sit right in the middle of it. There is no one who will come up and squeeze in next to you, unless they have been invited. Another interesting demarker of personal space involves the use of books, coats, and other personal possessions. Putting things on a chair or table clearly signifies that that space is taken. This happens in dayrooms, lounges, hospitals and nursing homes all the time. A variant on this behavior occurs when people establish a territory by constant use. Take as an example the person who has a favorite chair and feels comfortable telling anyone in it to get out. Other people also recognize this personal territory. Someone new on the ward would be told, not only by the person who holds that chair but also by other people in the room, that that is so-and-so's chair and that he better not sit there. It is fantastic the way we are acculturated to all of these spatial nuances and yet remain so insensitive to these phenomena in institutionalized patients.

DEFINING PRIVACY

This leads me to the broader issue of privacy (Postalan, 1970). Privacy, like territory, has a number of facets. I will deal with four of these facets. Basically, all four refer to the individual's ability to control the quality and quantity of his social interaction. The first facet of privacy is *solitude*, or the ability to have visual separation from other people. The second is *intimacy*, which involves a small group of people. Here it is possible to speak without fear that what is said will be communicated outside this group. *Anonymity* is the third facet. In this room, you are anonymous. You are sitting here watching other people's behavior, but you are not really concerned about it. You are not worried about your sense of privacy. The behavior we see in city parks where there are a lot of old people sitting around watching the streets and the pedestrians go by is another example of this type of privacy. The fourth facet is the condition of *reserve*. This is a psychological privacy necessitated when the physical surroundings do not permit the other levels of privacy. In essence, reserve is withdrawal into oneself. Dr. Arthur Schwartz, now at the Andrus Gerontology Center, formerly worked at the Veterans' Administration Hospital in Westwood. He observed a very interesting example of reserve among patients in the domiciliary there. The institution required that the men stay out of their dorm during certain hours of the day. They had to go out and find a place to relax or a place which they could use as a private space during the day. What often happened is that they would line up for meals two hours before mealtime. They had no other options but to stand in line. Many men in the line did not talk to each other. They were introverted into a state of reserve. How often do we mistake sullen inactivity for incompetence, when really it may be an adaptive escape into privacy? How often do we mistakingly label behavior with respect to personal possessions and furniture as eccentric, when, in fact, the person may be exercising the only territorial control he has available to him?

Privacy is very important for the individual. Everyone needs some sense of personal autonomy to avoid being constantly manipulated by the environment and to make decisions about what is public and what is not. The sense of emotional release is very much related to this. Our experiences during the day affect our mood. Our relationships with other people define us in different roles. If we are under the constant surveillance of other people, if we cannot change our physical setting to permit ourselves a respite from this surveillance, if we cannot move from one setting to another to change our roles or as our mode demands, we are forced to be always "on." People just can't do that every hour of the day. They need to be able to get off stage. They need a sense of privacy, which comes from moving from one situation into another in order to get emotional release. How often, I wonder, is the seemingly inappropriate behavior of a patient simply an outgrowth of his inability to match environments with his privacy needs? Imagine yourself cooped up in a small room or a building, 24 hours a day, for weeks on end, with a rotating shift of people always expecting you to be happy and cheerful? Isn't it reasonable to expect these people sometimes to be irritable if not contankerous? A greater consideration of these privacy needs in patients may help overcome some of the problems of institutionalization.

A less spacially bounded aspect of privacy is one of self-evaluation. That is, to be private enough from intrusion so that you can reflect on your experiences, and to catalogue what has been going on in a day. This quality of privacy is thought to be very important in maintaining a sense of "self."

AN APPLICATION OF THESE CONCEPTS

As a conclusion to this paper, I will illustrate how the notions of environment, psycho-social needs, territoriality and privacy can be applied to evaluate and improve institutional settings. There are innumerable movies, stories and novels that present us with images of stereotypic environments. The world is not constant as television programs and "Dr. Kildare" would have us think. There are hospitals where we find empty corridors and others where the corridors are crowded with people in wheelchairs or on benches. Often, there is a lot of social interaction going on, often there is not. The same thing happens in housing for the elderly, some spaces are extensively used by people, others are not. What is important here is that we are looking at an environment which, on a superficial basis, appears to be a constant. If you have seen one hospital corridor, you have seen them all, right? Wrong. In each of these settings the same behavior is not necessarily going on. The question is why? What environmental influences may be operative here? There can doubtless be many. For simplicity, let's just talk about furniture for a moment. If we have the furniture arranged in such a way that a few people can dominate it, other people will be kept out of that space. Why not try an experiment yourself just by changing chairs and couches around to see if you can improve the social functioning of a room or furniture arrangement? Also, generally in institutions, people tend to gravitate

CONTENTS

towards centers of activity. In a ward, patients like to cluster around the nursing station because there is something going on there. In the housing for the elderly, residents like to crowd around in the lounge or lobby because that is where the action is. Some of this grouping behavior may be prohibited by administrative policies, but often, it is also prohibited because we don't provide enough seating, or because we have architectural barriers that may hamper the mobility of the handicapped. Someone in a wheelchair, for example, may not be able to get over the bump where the floors and carpets interface. Spatial possessiveness is another factor which may limit access.

Understanding the relationship between the individual and the environment requires more than just looking at furniture. We have to try to trace behavior patterns back to their origin. We should examine other aspects of the individual's life within his setting. In what ways are we not allowing this person to develop a sense of privacy to protect his territoriality and to fulfill his psycho-social needs? A few years ago, I did a study of a park in Los Angeles used extensively by old people and of an adjacent retirement hotel. I found two startling things: (1) The people who came to the park on a regular basis came from apartments and private houses which had virtually no public spaces. These people wanted social interaction and had to go outside to get it. The park served as their living room. In the park, these people tended to be involved in socially intensive activities. (2) The people living in the retirement hotel were very different. Most of them didn't come to the park at all, and those that did, came to be alone or autonomous. They would just wander through the park. They did not get involved with other people and enjoy the excitement and natural setting around them. The hotel had a TV lounge, group dining, and an active lobby. In other words, the hotel had multiple places for social interaction. Residents didn't need to go outside for it.

This same kind of ecological relationship exists in institutions. Behavioral needs remain constant. What does change is the varied population of tenants placed in the available settings. A study done a few years ago at the Philadelphia Geriatric Center (Lawton, 1970) provides a very clear demonstration of the ecological relationship between spatial settings within the institutional context. Originally, the ward which was studied consisted of a number of six-bed units. Patients had virtually no private space within the six-bed unit to which they were assigned. During the day, these people would sit in chairs in the corridor outside their room. These chairs were used and defended as personal possessions. The patients themselves were reserved so that very little social interaction went on in the corridor. In fact, little public use was made of the corridor because to go down it, it was necessary constantly to cross territorial boundaries. Understandably, the lounge area at the end of the corridor was rarely used.

Then, something unusual happened. The physical environment was modified, and behavior patterns were monitored. The rooms were changed into six cubicle units instead of open rooms. The corridor wall was opened into a half-wall. Interesting things happened as a result of these changes. The cubicles became a very private space. The area between the cubicle and the room's half-wall became a living room or porch into which other patients would be invited. Patients stopped using their chairs in the corridors as a private refuge and the ward lounge area became more active. The point of all this is that a series of spatial behaviors were linked and modified by changing one aspect of the setting, the six-bed arrangement. Changing the physical environment will not always solve problems existing on a ward or in an institution, but it is a starting place.

The physical setting is the framework in which people can act. People have diverse needs. Fulfillment of these needs may require access to a variety of spatial settings. When I worked in a hospital geriatric ward, we almost never took our patients outside, not even on the porch. We kept them constrained in their beds all day long. If for some "unexplainable" reason they became agitated or restless, they were tranquilized. Perhaps changing their environment would have been a better remedy.

To summarize, let me reiterate that the environment is a complex phenomena made up of the individual, the physical setting, the rules and regulations governing that setting and the people in it, and our interpersonal and suprapersonal social constants. When we are concerned with environmental influences on behavior, we must be aware of its complexity. We must also be aware of the psycho-social needs of the individual for order, identity, social connectedness, and effectance. Matching the environment to these needs is not an easy task. We can begin by being sensitive to the implications of our action and motion, and by making full use of the alternatives open to us.

REFERENCES

Bengston, V.L. and Kuypers, J. Psycho-social needs and dying: Connectedness and effectance throughout the life cycle. Paper presented at the 15th Annual Meeting of the Western Gerontological Society. Oct. 10, 1969, Los Angeles.

Hall, E.T. *The Hidden Dimension.* New York: Doubleday and Co., 1966.

Lawton, P. Ecology and Aging. In L. Pastalan and D. Carson (Eds.), *Special Behavior of Older People,* Ann Arbor: University of Michigan Press, 1970.

MacDonald, A. and Newcomer, R. Influences in Perception of a City Park as a Supportive or Threatening Environment. In D. Grady and D. Pelegrind (Eds.), *Reflections on the Recreation and Park Movement,* Iowa: William C. Brown Co., 1973.

Pastalan, L. Privacy as an Expression of Human Territoriality. In L. Pastalan and D. Carson (Eds.), Spatial Behavior of Older People, Ann Arbor: University of Michigan Press, 1970.

Shaw, D. Cultural Shock, P.O.W.'s Return: Big Adjustment to Little Things. In *Los Angeles Times,* part 1, p. 1+, Saturday, Feb. 3, 1973.

IX ETHNICITY, SOCIAL POLICY AND AGING

Barbara Solomon, D.S.W.*

My first job was on a geriatric ward. I discovered it was great because nobody else was interested and I could do almost anything I wanted to. Because nobody ever told me I couldn't do things I wanted to, I had such a good sense of creative and innovative potential in my work.

I think that when we look at why we get into the jobs we do, we must understand that all behavior is multi-determined. One of the good things about working at the U.S.C. Gerontology Center is that there are so many wonderful behavioral scientists interested in the intricacies of the human condition. But like all behavioral scientists, we sometimes forget that we are studying ourselves at the same time we are studying the concerns of our disciplines. There have to be subjective reasons for our choosing the field that we do. There are some very subjective reasons why so many of us are here today, thinking about aging. Aging, as an issue, is becoming more and more recognized in our society. We are lucky if we already recognize that we will grow old.

I have had the frustration of dealing with graduate students in the School of Social Work in a course called, "Human Behavior in a Social Environment," and of having them move away from me as soon as we got to the aging stage of the life cycle. Up to that time, they were a very involved group. As we started dealing with the issues of old age, I began to feel them practically leaving the room. Most of the time when confronted with what was happening, they gave me answers like, "I know I'll never be psychotic, so I don't mind working with psychotics. But working with aging people always reminds me that I am going to be old, and I don't want to think about that now."

This is what has been happening in our society. Aging has been something we don't want to think about. The whole Gerontology Center operation is a testimony to the fact that we not only have to think about aging, but we have to think about it in a very systematic way if we are going to understand the issues we have to solve. Old age concerns all of us.

We have to see aging as part of the total life system. Academicians like to put things in boxes. Then they label the boxes with names like biology, and sociology, and psychology. I like to tell my behavioral scientist colleagues that we social

**Associate Professor of Social Work, University of Southern California, Los Angeles*

workers have to put the parts all back together again as we try to deal with the whole person.

It is necessary to see the concerns of older people in the context of all the concerns that people in our country have at this time. What happens to people in any human system, in any society, is based primarily on the nature of the political processes. No matter how we can analyze the consequences of human behavior, we have to understand the political processes that do not permit us total control over the conditions of our lives. It's ironic that two large age groups, the young and the old, are vying for the rewards and resources of society at the same time in very intensive kinds of ways. At about the same time that we have a youth movement pushing and pressing for more involvement, we have older people saying that they want to be more involved, to have more control over their lives, and to have more of the resources of society allocated to them. The racial ethnic groups are also making demands on society. All of this is taking place simultaneously in what someone called "the cultural prison break." So, what we have is an interesting social mixture of Black power and senior power vying for the resources of government and for the attention of practitioners.

Again, it is necessary to be able to look at the total system. I am particularly concerned with the ways that ethnic elderly are able to tie into the concerns of academicians. A lot of research literature does not really concern itself with the heterogeneity around us, but looks for the model behaviors, the model groups, and the model profiles. There has even been a kind of philosophical bent in our society to consider and talk only about the dominant group, the Anglo group in our society. And, we talk about assimilation and acculturation as if all other groups should aspire to the model the Anglo group poses for our society. I prefer to believe that we must go even beyond the idea of cultural pluralism (that is, different groups on different tracks in our society), but realize that we do have different cultural groups that are constantly influencing each other. The idea has been that if you move away from your own ethnic group, somehow you move toward the Anglo group in terms of cultural norms, and soon. If we are constantly in interaction with each other, we have to have some sense of the value of uniqueness, the value of the heterogeneity, and the value of the diversity. This is necessary so that we do not look subserviently to the Anglo group and beg for resources, but we look to the Anglo group as peers and as the bigger brother in the family who has been hogging all the resources. Now we want our part. In terms of ethnicity and aging, this suggests some very important ideas that need to be discussed.

To what extent is ethnicity an important factor when we

begin to look at elderly persons and their social functioning? We have felt a great deal of pressure in the universities to include more ethnic content in the curriculum. In many cases, it has been a kind of add-on. I see this as not very productive. All of us are human beings first, and there is no such thing as Black psychology or Chicano psychology. We do not have to re-invent the wheel. There are theoretical perspectives on human behavior that are universal. However, what we have not done is to assert the significance of the heterogeneity of the human condition when we looked at these theoretical perspectives in the past.

There is a different perspective from the academic point of view than from that of the practitioner. The practitioner is constantly faced with the individual. No matter what you may say he must do, you are faced with what this one human being you are dealing with at a given time does. It is important to look for generalizations, but the social scientists use their generalizations in a very different way than we practitioners do. Social scientists do their research and they come up with generalizations, or hypotheses for further studies. Practitioners go to this literature and take out these generalizations as prescriptions for action. On this basis, we behave in various types of ways toward people. It is extremely important that we, as practitioners, look at what the social scientists have generated, particularly as it relates to ethnic groups and see what is usable and what still needs to be done. A great deal needs to be done.

There does seem to be certain theoretical perspectives that I think can help us to understand what some of the differences might be when we look at people of different ethnic groups. I almost hesitate to say "theoretical" to people who are practitioners. In teaching a graduate course that is highly theoretical, I hear students say that they are sick of all this theory, that they have theory up to here, that they want action, that they want to go out and change things, and that they don't see where all that theory is really very helpful. In this new day in colleges and universities, you try to be very responsive to students. They practically had me so convinced about theory that I was afraid to say Freud's name. Students are particularly hostile towards anything analytic, and I had partly erased theory from my comments. I do think that there is this tendency because the problems are so great and because there are so many pressing issues that need resolution right now. We feel so pressed that it is extremely difficult for us sometimes to step back from these problems and look at theoretical perspectives that might have some answer, or that might give us a lead toward the solution of a problem. For most of the research about human behavior, which is research done primarily in the dominant community, the findings may be very valid. Whenever you talk about these findings, you are talking about a set of probabilities for any given situation and saying that people in this situation are more likely to do one thing than something else. For the different ethnic groups, it is the probabilities that may be different. I think these are things that we need to be very concerned with.

Another of the things I am concerned about is the way we look at the whole integration process in our society. Most of us will agree that we live in isolation from each other. In one of my classes, I had a map of the area. I stuck pins at the addresses where the white students lived and the non-whites lived. I could draw a straight line, without any gerrymandering, so that the blacks were on one side and the whites were on the other. This can be repeated over and over again in our society. We are isolated from each other and therefore we do not have a good understanding, in many cases, of another person's lifestyle, the conditions that impinge on him, his priorities, and his concerns. As a way of dealing with this as a social goal, we have got to have a more integrated society. For the most part, integration is good. Unfortunately there have been times when the means have obscured what the ends are. We have used integration as a way of dealing with problems, and sometimes it is imposed in a situation where it creates more problems than it actually resolves.

I feel very strongly that, for the older person particularly, continuity in lifestyle is something of extreme importance. No person should be thrown into situations and conditions which are alien if they are to make an adequate adjustment. And yet, in our society right now, social policy dictates that all institutions must be integrated. They must try to achieve this at all costs. I think these are stringent dictates placed on institutions especially when many times the ends are not being satisfied by this particular means. There is a very interesting nursing home in Los Angeles which is predominantly Japanese-American. The staff is Japanese; they can give Japanese type baths; the food is Japanese, and so on. Certainly the older Japanese-American who goes into that kind of institutional setting is going to make a much more adequate adjustment, from my point of view, than if he had been placed in an all-Anglo institution. Now, this does not mean that this instituion will only take Japanese. Certainly an Anglo who had grown up in a Japanese community, might be very much at ease with that lifestyle. It is an option that he has. The best society is one which offers the most options so people can actually gratify their needs rather than one which establishes some kind of universal that everybody has to conform to. By recognizing

94

and understanding the significance of culture in the lives of people, we can more adequately begin to develop a social policy to support this necessary continuity in lifestyle.

There are some other issues in the literature of particular significance to people of different ethnic groups. There is much research in aging that has been directed toward retirement. For many older Blacks, for example, the concept of retirement doesn't even exist so that much of this literature does not even apply. It is only recently that many Blacks, who have been able to get more stable jobs, may be actually facing retirement. I find a great deal of resistance to retirement among these older Blacks. This resistance is not so much because of what has been said in the retirement literature about fear of loss of status, and so on. The resistance seems to result from these tremendous changes going on in their occupational status. There are more opportunities than ever before, and for the first time, they may be actually getting an equitable kind of salary. And, having reached this new and higher level, they are being told to get out! By their resistance they are saying, "This is what I have really worked to achieve all of these years. Now that I am reaching these goals, you are telling me I have got to leave."

I think there is also a great deal of concern about the different impact of retirement on men than on women in the dominant group. The job has been probably the largest component of identity for males, whereas for women, their identity has been not so much with the job (because many women didn't work), but with their marriage. In many ethnic groups, there has not been the same kind of structuring of family economy. Most Black women have always worked. Therefore, retirement for Black women is a very different kind of thing, compared to retirement for white women. Many of the issues that deal with family structure need to be looked at in terms of ethnic groups and the whole concept of the extended family. I feel that a truism in our society is that most ethnic racial minorities have experienced more extended family ties than has the dominant group. At least that's what we are told. Of course, there is always the issue of whether this has been for the most part cultural or situational. That is, if the dominant society is not providing major kinds of support, then this has been the family's responsibility. Will this particular kind of extended family interaction continue if the larger society becomes more responsive to the needs of that particular group? I grew up in the South, and whenever we went somewhere, we stayed with relatives because we couldn't stay at a motel or hotel. I am wondering whether this same kind of pattern will continue for very long with the new laws. I know things tend to change slowly, but I have heard a lot of grumbling among our relatives who had people coming in and who thought, "Why don't they go to a motel or hotel?" They don't because this has not been their life experience. This is particularly true for older relatives in the nonwhite groups. I don't think you can encourage them to go to hotels and motels at this late date. These are issues that need a great deal of attention by the social science researchers.

The vulnerability of racial and ethnic groups to being uprooted in our society is a tremendous concern to me. Again, from the standpoint of behavioral science theory, a basic human need is to have some kind of place, space and time that we can call our own. This is true, even if we live in an institution. It is awful when beds are moved around at the whim of the staff. In a community, we would not like our homes to be bulldozed to be replaced by a highrise building. I think that the racial and ethnic minorities have been particularly vulnerable. In the past and even now, they have had no power to deal with the public bodies that make decisions about who will move and who will not. Freeways slice through their communities and urban renewal projects uproot them to build buildings they cannot afford to live in. These are the concerns that we must deal with in developing social policies that will protect the rights of all people in our society.

As a practitioner, I think it is critical that we have an acute awareness of how the people we are dealing with have lived in the past, what their priorities are, what their values are, and where they want to go. And, in the kind of racist society we live in, this is extremely difficult. I have been amazed at the naivete of some of my white students in the School of Social Work who honestly will say, "I think I have a marvellous relationship with all of my Black clients. I hear fewer complaints from them than from my white clients." You have to look at the significance of this more critically. This client is a person who may be really full of anger and hatred and who is not letting you in on his real feelings. If you are privy to these feelings, how can you really be helpful to him? A great deal has to be done to help the practitioner be sensitive to how his client is feeling about him and how his client is responding to the kinds of things he is doing. When I went to Berkeley, I learned that it was important to "love one another." If you didn't, and if you dared come up with anything that might have been considered prejudicial, then you might easily get counseled out of school. It was thought that all you had to do to be able to work with other people was to feel that they are all "valuable human beings." To quote an old cliche: "The road to Hell is paved with good intentions." There are those of us who really do want to do the best thing for other people, but if you don't know, and you don't understand how others are thinking and feeling about you, then all the good intentions in the world will not help you.

I think practitioners operate with a great deal of myth about their influence during their interaction with people of different races or ethnic groups. These myths need exploding, particularly as we work with elderly people. Very often, they are living the past in the present. We may project what is happening in the present into their lives when, in effect, it is not as accurate description of the way they think, or feel, or want to be in this world. It is extremely important that we understand their world. We must not only understand it by trying to help older people make the best possible adjustment that they can make, we must also look toward the future ourselves and envision the kind of world we would like to have in our old age. We must decide what has to be done now to have that world in the future. Many of the older people now are living what they are and what they have been and what they will forever be. We cannot try to change them as a way of changing the future. Once we understand this, we can enter their life and can be a great deal more helpful to them.

Let me re-emphasize that social policy is the way the federal government, city governments, state governments, and agencies set forth desirable social goals, which influence the development of special programs for people. I think that to have an enlightened society, we need more basic kinds of research, particularly in the area of ethnicity and aging. This is necessary if we are going to create a society that will support the effective adjustment of all older people to the world they have to live in.

X PUTTING IT ALL TOGETHER:
Challenge and Commitment to the Aged

*Theodore Koff, Ed.D.**

As I reflect on these papers, a couple of themes are evident. One is that there is significant value simply in getting new information. Perhaps this information helps to break down the protective nest surrounding us. It challenges us to reexamine what we've been doing. We have been challenged by the new ideas, the new thinking, and the new research represented by these papers. Hopefully this will enable us to move into a new kind of professionalism in dealing with the problems we face. Questions are raised here about the differences between illness and aging. The continuity of the aging process has been stressed, and the attempt has been made to disassociate illness and aging. Also, we now feel the importance of knowing accurately, of getting information from the research findings that are available to us.

These papers have been an educational experience for me. One of the primary purposes of education is change. If there is a change in our own expectations as a result of this new information about older people and about illness and health, then how can we modify our behavior so that it will be more appropriate? Our behavior should be modified in a way that gives the older person more responsibility. We know older people have the capacity for responsibility. It is important to communicate new information so that we can use this information to change our expectations, our relationships, and our regard for older people. I'd like to put it in the context of some kind of perceptual change. We need to change the way we see our relationships and ourselves working with older people. We must identify positively with new bases of knowledge and then bring together the best we have in planning programs for the aged. We have to have an active engagement in the kinds of changes that have to evolve, not just an identification through reading the newspaper or the professional journal.

One of the reasons I relate to the content of these papers is that I have an active identification with older people. I am an administrator of a home for the aged, a long-term care facility and community outpatient program. I also am an educator at the University of Arizona. I am also a child of aged parents, and I am an aging person.

Executive Director, Handmaker Jewish Nursing Home for the Aged, Tucson, Arizona.

I think there is a crisis in our society now. I think there is a crisis which affects the nature of the services that we are able to offer to older people. I think this crisis attacks the concept that we can do for each other better than what an individual can do for himself. I think this crisis attacks the possibility of collectively coming together and studying and training people, and using our resources in the best way for all people. There is, I sense, an underlying and developing crisis that is attacking the concepts and the progress we've made in the last ten years. It is prohibiting us from building a kind of society that has a much brighter and greater potential for older people. I see it from these personal perspectives I have just listed.

As an administrator of a home, I am concerned about having continuing sources of funds that will enable us to meet present and future standards. We haven't reached the pinnacle level of care in the institutional setting. We cannot stop at this point and and say that the funding we have available is adequate to do the jobs we know how to do for people in our community. We must bring more money; we must bring more research; we must bring better programs and better use of the existing resources to develop good environments for older people within our society. These are my concerns as an administrator.

I want us to develop the best quality of care that we can. I think there is challenge now. There is the challenge of alternatives in institutional care. But clearly, institutions are appropriate for those people who need them, and these institutions must provide the highest quality of services that can be made available for them. I also direct an outpatient program that serves about 300 people in the community. These are 300 people who come from the poorest homes, from the poorest sections of the community. Their new ray of light has come not from our commitment saying, "Yes, we ought to do something," but from federal money. This money has actualized our plans into food, activities, recreation, health care, and meaningful existence for this group of people in our community. But now the very subsistence of these people is challenged by threats to the continuity of these essential funds.

What are our alternatives then? I don't think we ought to panic because we are threatened. What do we do as a result of these threats? We must organize our thinking and redouble our efforts. We have to pull together the very best to find new resources wherever possible so we can continue to have good programs. What does all this mean to me as an educator? I've begun to seek a life for the aging within our whole campus setting. We want to introduce into other parts of our curriculum more thinking about aging. This has been stimulated and promoted by the availability of resources and funds enabling people to study in the field. What are the alternatives here? Are we going to say that because federal support for the continuity of some programs might be threatened, that the cumulative effect of the past years will be washed out? I hope that we are going to say that the things we have experienced over the past years will enable us to regroup. We need to contain the best thinking we have and to look at resource alternatives that need to be developed. I don't think we need to continue the meetings we've had searching for alternatives to institutional care. I think we have to develop alternative directions to efforts in aging. Maybe we need to have a conference around that kind of theme.

I also want to react as a child of aged parents. I think the most important way we look at the challenge on aging today is from our own level. We are each involved in this. We are concerned for our fellow man, for our communities, and for the people who live there. We've demonstrated a commitment to a way of life in our community for older people. We've developed, I think, a oneness in our concern for the aged. We are really the ones who are keyed to making all of this happen. We can put it together in our agency setting, in the places where we work, with the staff we work with, with the boards at our agencies, with the way we spend the money and the way we care for our people. We can put it together for ourselves in our professional settings, in the way we show a concern for the aged, and in the way we work with them. We can put it together in our educational system in the way it can enhance the productive use of the knowledge we have. We can put it together on our local governmental levels and on a national level. If we really resolve for ourselves the kinds of reasons why we are in aging and what we want to do about it, then we can finally put it together in a whole package.